ISSUES THAT CONCERN YOU

Teen Suicide

Heidi Williams, *Book Editor*

GREENHAVEN PRESS

A part of Gale, Cengage Learning

GALE
CENGAGE Learning

Detroit • New York • San Francisco • New Haven, Conn • Waterville, Maine • London

Christine Nasso, *Publisher*
Elizabeth Des Chenes, *Managing Editor*

Articles in Greenhaven Press anthologies are often edited for length to meet page requirements. In addition, original titles of these works are changed to clearly present the main thesis and to explicitly indicate the author's opinion. Every effort is made to ensure that Greenhaven Press accurately reflects the original intent of the authors. Every effort has been made to trace the owners of copyrighted material.

Cover image copyright Dave Greenberg, 2009. Used under license from Shutterstock.com.

LIBRARY OF CONGRESS CATALOGING-IN-PUBLICATION DATA

Teen suicide / Heidi Williams, book editor.
   p. cm. -- (Issues that concern you)
 Includes bibliographical references and index.
 ISBN 978-0-7377-4497-2 (hardcover)
 1. Teenagers--Suicidal behavior--United States. 2. Suicide--United States--Prevention.
I. Williams, Heidi.
 HV6546.T4139 2009
 362.280835'0973--dc22
                                                    2009016632

Printed in the United States of America
1 2 3 4 5 6 7 13 12 11 10 09

CONTENTS

INTRODUCTION

In 2005, about 30,000 people in the United States were killed with a gun. About 2 percent of those were either legal killings, like by the police in emergency situations, or were of undetermined intent. Three percent were gun accidents. Forty percent were homicides. The rest—the majority, about 55 percent—were suicides. These statistics are nothing new. From 1980 to 2005, in four out of every five years, suicides accounted for more gun-related deaths than murders and accidents combined. During these years, if you were killed by a gun, most likely you pulled the trigger yourself.

The pervasiveness of violence toward self extends beyond gunfire, however. In 2005, more than 50,000 people in the United States died a violent death. Again, the majority of these homicides were not from drive-by shootings, robberies, or hits. They were not committed by thugs, crazed junkies, angry spouses, or jilted lovers. They were by our own hands. Of the 50,000 violent deaths in the United States each year, the majority—more than 32,000—are suicides. For every two suicides we hear about in the evening news, there are 3 suicides somewhere out there. Furthermore, in school-age children, for every 1 suicide there are an estimated 100 to 200 attempts.

The pervasiveness of violence toward self also extends beyond our borders. According to the World Health Organization (WHO), annually about 2 million people die violent deaths. About half of these—1 million—are suicides. Worldwide, more people die from suicide than from murder and war combined. Furthermore, according to WHO, "Estimates suggest fatalities could rise to 1.5 million by 2020." As high as the numbers of suicides are, the attempts are far greater. Worldwide an estimated 10 to 20 million people fail at attempted suicides annually.

The effects of violence toward self also extend far beyond self. In a study conducted in 2007 by the Violence Policy Center, at least 554 people in the United States died in murder-suicides during

About 1 million people worldwide commit suicide annually, and another estimated 10 to 20 million attempt suicide.

the first half of that year in cases ranging from domestic violence to the Virginia Tech massacre. Of these 554 murder-suicide deaths, 234 (42 percent) were suicides and 320 (58 percent) were homicides. Suicide can be more than doubly violent. As one medical professional states, "Because many murder-suicides result in the death or injury of family members and sometimes mass murder, they cause countless additional morbidity, family trauma, and disruption of communities."

In fact, suicidal murderers may be more lethal than mere murderers. This is perhaps most evident in the school shootings of recent years. Of the 41 major school shooting cases from 1997 to 2007, 28 involved murder or attempted murder only, while only 6 cases involved suicide or attempted suicide only, and only 7 were murder-suicides. There were by far more homicidal events;

however, while in the 28 murder cases, 26 people were murdered and 66 were injured, in the seven murder-suicide cases, 31 people were murdered and 44 were injured. Seven murder-suicide events involving 8 gunmen proved more lethal than 28 gunmen attempting murder only. Furthermore, these figures do not include university shootings, such as the Virginia Tech massacre in April of 2007 in which 1 gunman killed 32 people and wounded more than 20 before turning the gun on himself.

Despite the prevalence of suicide over homicide, homicide seems to receive more media attention than suicide. The Violence Policy Center report on murder-suicide states, regarding the Virginia Tech massacre, "In the inevitable analysis following such tragic events, attention is rarely given to the fact that many such mass shootings are in fact murder-suicides." Benjamin Radford, managing editor of *Skeptical Inquirer* science magazine, writes, "One reason that people believe homicide is much more common than suicide is because of the news media's selective coverage. . . . While murders make daily news, suicides and suicide attempts are often not considered newsworthy unless the victim is famous."

Others say that we are reluctant to talk about the issue of suicide, hoping that ignoring it will make it go away. However, according to Saul Wilen, a physician and developer of a school suicide prevention program, "There seems to be a universal fear that if you talk about them [suicides] they will occur more, that if you put it in the closet there's no more problem. What we've found is that if you put it in the closet it's actually a bigger problem."

Authors in this anthology examine teen suicide from a variety of perspectives. In addition, the volume contains several appendixes to help the reader understand and explore the topic, including a thorough bibliography and a list of organizations to contact for further information. The appendix titled "What You Should Know About Teen Suicide" offers vital facts about suicide and how it affects young people. The appendix "What You Should Do About Teen Suicide" offers information for young people confronted with this issue. With all these features, *Issues That Concern You: Teen Suicide* is an excellent resource on this important topic.

ONE

Teen Suicide Is a Significant Problem

Nationwide Children's Hospital

> *NewsRx Health & Science* is a weekly publication that summarizes the most significant research being done in U.S. universities and research centers. This article summarizes a study first reported in the *Journal of the American Medical Association* that identified a sudden and large increase in the number of adolescent suicides in the United States after many years of decline.

A troubling study in the September 3rd [2008] *Journal of the American Medical Association* [JAMA] raises new concerns about kids committing suicide in this country. After a one year spike in the number of suicides, doctors were hoping to see more normal numbers in the latest study, but they didn't. The number of kids committing suicide in the U.S. remains higher than expected, and that has doctors and parents looking for answers.

For more than a decade the suicide rate among kids in this country had steadily and consistently declined, but that trend ended abruptly.

"Suddenly in 2004 we see the sharpest increase in the past 15 years and it appears that it's persisting into 2005," says Jeff Bridge, PhD, Nationwide Children's Hospital.

Suicide, Considered or Attempted: Rates Among U.S. High School Students, 2005

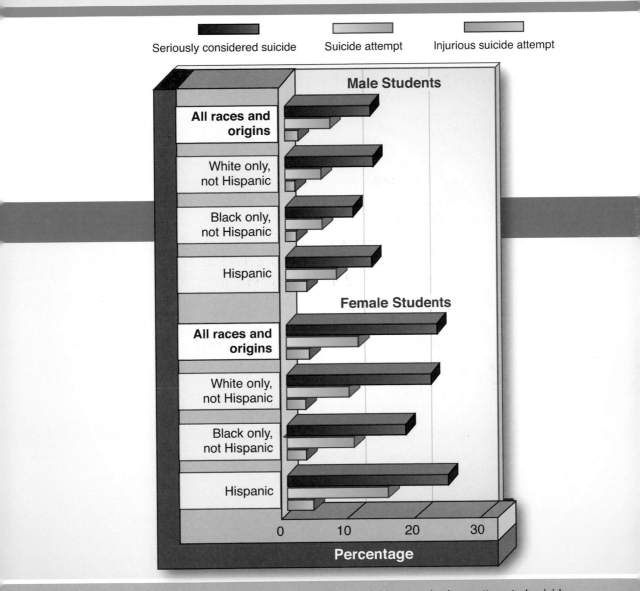

Some students who seriously considered suicide may also have attempted suicide. An injurious suicide attempt resulted in an injury, poisoning, or overdose that was treated by a doctor or nurse.

Taken from: A.P. MacKay and C. Duran, *Adolescent Health in the United States, 2007*. National Center for Health Statistics. 2007. Centers for Disease Control and Prevention, National Center for Chronic Disease. Youth Risk Behavior Survey. www.cdc.gov/nchs/data/misc/adolescent2007.pdf.

2005 is the most recent year that the numbers are available, and they don't look promising. Jeff Bridge is a researcher at Nationwide Children's Hospital who conducted the study. He says while the numbers dipped slightly between '04 and '05 overall they are still up significantly.

That's disturbing news to Rick Baumann. After his son, Gabe, first attempted suicide as a teenager, Rick devoted his life to suicide prevention and educating others. Like many parents, Rick knew little about warning signs.

"He just withdrew, wasn't answering phone calls to his friends and all of that, but I have four other children and he was a teenager, and I just assumed it was teenage behavior," says Rick.

The Cause Is Undetermined

But often it's much more than that, and now that researchers have identified what may be an emerging crisis, the next step is to figure out what's causing it. One answer may lie in the prescription of antidepressant medication. Because of concerns over side effects, the number of kids prescribed anti-depressants has dropped by as much as 20 percent and that may be having a dire impact.

"The vast majority of young people who complete suicide have some sort of psychiatric disorder. Most commonly depression or some mood disorder," says John Campo, MD, Nationwide Children's Hospital.

So the kids who need the medicine most may not be getting it. Campo says there is no proven link between the drop in prescriptions and the rise in suicides, but the fact that they happened at the same time is worth looking into. Experts say they also want to look into the Internet and how that may be playing a role in the number of kids committing suicide.

Following a decade of steady decline, the suicide rate among U.S. youth younger than 20 years of age increased by 18 percent from 2003–2004—the largest single-year change in the pediatric suicide rate over the past 15 years. Although worrisome, the one-year spike observed in 2003–2004 does not necessarily reflect a changing trend. Therefore, researchers examined national data on youth suicide from 1996–2005 in order to determine whether the increase persisted from 2004–2005, the latest year for which data are available.

Researchers estimated the trend in suicide rates from 1996–2003 using log-linear regression. Using that trend line, they estimated the expected suicide rates in 2004 and 2005 and compared

The majority of teens who commit suicide have some sort of psychiatric disorder, such as depression or a mood disorder.

the expected number of deaths to the actual observed number of deaths. Researchers found that although the overall observed rate of suicide among 10 to 19 year olds decreased by about 5 percent between 2004 and 2005 (the year following the spike) both the 2004 and 2005 rates were still significantly greater than the expected rates, based on the 1996–2003 trend.

A Public Health Crisis

"The fact that this significant increase in pediatric suicides continued into 2005 implies that the alarming spike witnessed from 2003–2004 was more than just a single-year anomaly," said Jeff Bridge, PhD, lead author and a principal investigator in The Research Institute at Nationwide Children's Hospital. "We now need to consider the possibility that the increase is an indicator of an emerging public health crisis."

In order to understand the possible causes behind the increase in youth suicides between 2003 and 2005, researchers say additional studies must be conducted.

"Identifying the risk factors associated with pediatric suicide is an important next step," said Joel Greenhouse, PhD, Professor of Statistics at Carnegie Mellon University and a co-author of the study.

Several factors that should be considered as possible contributors to the increase in youth suicides include the influence of Internet social networks, increases in suicide among U.S. troops and higher rates of untreated depression in the wake of recent "black box" warnings on antidepressants—a possible unintended consequence of the medication warnings required by the Federal Drug Administration in 2004. Researchers stress that, whatever the explanation, effective interventions to reduce pediatric suicides must be addressed nationally.

TWO

Gay Teens Are at Greater Risk for Suicide

Tim Murphy

> Tim Murphy is a former editor and writer for *Poz*, a magazine chronicling the HIV epidemic and supporting its victims. He also writes for *The New York Times* and *New York Magazine*. Murphy wrote the following article for *The Advocate*, a national gay and lesbian newsmagazine. In this article he discusses the recent spike in youth suicides and examines the resulting implications for the suicide rate of gay youth, which according to some experts and studies, is significantly higher than the suicide rate of the general youth population.

At 20, Jacob Breslow, a junior at the University of California, Santa Cruz, is thriving. Right now he's part of a field-study program in London, where he's taking part in the United Kingdom's LGBT [Lesbian, Gay, Bisexual, and Transgender/Transexual] History Month. "I want to be a professor of queer theory, identity, and culture," he says confidently.

Things weren't always so great. Six years ago, in his hometown of Walnut Creek, California, an affluent suburb east of San Francisco, Breslow felt so ostracized after coming out during his freshman year of high school that he twice tried to kill himself.

Tim Murphy, "Stormy Weather: This Fall the CDC Reported the Greatest Spike in the Number of Teen Suicides in 15 Years. What Does This Mean for Gay Youths?" *The Advocate*, October 23, 2007. Reproduced by permission.

"The worst part for me was the isolation and thinking nobody cared, paired with people saying awful comments and teachers not doing anything," Breslow recalls.

The number of young people who have been in the straits once faced by Jacob made headlines in September [2007], when the Centers for Disease Control and Prevention [CDC] reported that suicide rates among those ages 10 to 24 rose 8% from 2003 to 2004, the largest rise in 15 years. Some experts attributed the spike to a decline in antidepressant use among young people after the U.S. Food and Drug Administration issued warnings in 2003 and 2004 that they could increase the incidence of suicidal thoughts or actions in that age group.

So just how many of those young people were LGBT? According to a CDC spokesperson, the data examined didn't reveal sexual orientation. However, numerous studies—particularly the anonymous Youth Risk Behavior Surveys [YRBSs] from the handful of states and cities that ask participants about their sexual orientation—have found suicide ideation to be far more common among LGBT youths than among the broader youth population.

Gay Teens Are Still at Risk

If you think that an increasingly gay-friendly culture and a recent blossoming of resources for young gay people has led to a declining suicide risk in that group, think again. As recently as 2005 a Youth Risk Behavior Survey of 3,522 students in relatively pro-gay Massachusetts found that sexual-minority adolescents were 2.5 times more likely than their straight peers to have hurt themselves on purpose, three times as likely to have seriously considered suicide, and four times as likely to have attempted it.

"I don't believe that suicide ideation has decreased because the culture is more accepting," says Charles Robbins, executive director of the Trevor Project, a nationwide crisis and suicide-prevention hotline for gay youths that he says receives more than 12,000 calls a year. "The majority of our calls come from outside large metropolitan areas," many of them from smaller communities in the Midwest and the South.

Recent surveys show that gay teens are two-and-a-half times more likely to hurt themselves than their straight peers.

"It's not about seeing an open lifestyle on TV," Robbins explains. "When they're at home in a small town and petrified about coming out, not a lot has changed."

But studies that have found dramatically higher rates of suicidal thoughts or attempts among LGBT youths have a critic in Ritch Savin-Williams, a Cornell University professor and author of *The*

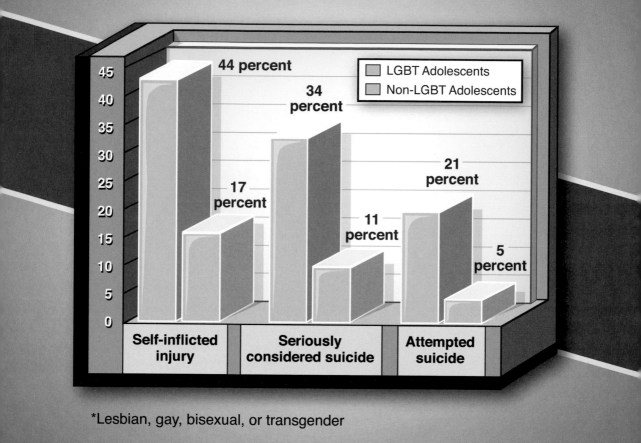

Suicide Rates Are Much Greater for LGBT* Adolescents

Legend: LGBT Adolescents / Non-LGBT Adolescents

Self-inflicted injury: 44 percent / 17 percent

Seriously considered suicide: 34 percent / 11 percent

Attempted suicide: 21 percent / 5 percent

*Lesbian, gay, bisexual, or transgender

Taken from: *2005 Massachusetts Youth Risk Behavior Survey Results: Executive Summary*, Massachusetts Department of Education, June 2006. www.doe.mass.edu/cnp/hprograms/yrbs/o5/ch6.pdf.

New Gay Teenager. He says that most such studies count only youths who identify as LGBT at an early age and are often therefore more vulnerable than those who may have same-sex feelings but don't yet identify as LGBT. "Same-sex-attracted youth are just as healthy as any other kid," he says. "I think we need to back off some of our negative messages."

More Data Are Coming

That may be harder to do next year [2008], when a study conducted by San Francisco State University's Cesar Chavez Institute is expected to be released. Researchers talked to a cross-section of LGBT youths and their families throughout California to correlate the relationship between family reactions to a child's being LGBT and the child's risk of events including HIV infection, substance abuse, depression, and suicide ideation.

Study leader Caitlin Ryan was guarded about the results but insists that the study provides the most detailed evidence to date of a link between family rejection and suicide.

Parents were "shocked," Ryan says, and "in tears" when they learned "that they could play a role in causing their children to think of taking their own lives." Researchers talked to parents, including those from immigrant households, who wouldn't let their LGBT children sit with them in church, walk on the street with them, or visit relatives with them.

On the other hand, Ryan adds, the study also found evidence of tremendous resilience among LGBT youths as well as willingness among parents to change their attitudes and embrace their gay children.

It was resilience that helped Breslow recover after his second suicide attempt. "I looked around and said, 'I'm not going to take this anymore; I'm worth way more than anyone here who's judging me,'" he recalls. He joined a network of young LGBT activists in the Bay Area, taking on work that led to his receiving funding in 2007 from the Point Foundation, an organization that supports exceptional young LGBT scholars.

Gone is his old view that no one cared and his life wouldn't improve. "Now it's just a strict look to the future," says Breslow, "me saying, Where can we go from here and what can we do that's positive?"

THREE

Native American Teens Are at Greater Risk for Suicide

Jerry Gidner

> Jerry Gidner, an enrolled member of the Sault Ste. Marie Tribe of Chippewa Indians in Michigan, has worked in the U.S. Department of the Interior for the Bureau of Indian Affairs (BIA) and Office of Indian Affairs since 1998 and was appointed director of the BIA in 2007. In 2006, as deputy bureau director for Tribal Services, he testified before the Committee on Indian Affairs at the U.S. Senate Hearing on the Establishment of Suicide Prevention Programs and Their Application in Indian Country. In this viewpoint, his testimony, he explains the magnitude of the problem of suicide among Native American young people and how federal funding would help continue programs that work toward solving this ongoing crisis.

Teen suicide is a serious long-standing problem in Indian country. Research has shown that social factors such as poverty, alcoholism, gangs, and violence contribute in the manifestation of suicidal ideation, suicidal behavior and suicide attempts by Indian children and teenagers.

Jerry Gidner, "Testimony of Jerry Gidner, Deputy Bureau Director for Tribal Services, Bureau of Indian Affairs, U.S. Department of the Interior Before the Committee on Indian Affairs," *United States Senate Hearing on the Establishment of an* [sic] *Suicide Prevention Programs and their Application in Indian Country,* May 17, 2006. Reproduced by permission.

The Indian Health Service [IHS] data document [indicates] that suicide is the 3rd leading cause of death in Indian children age 5 to 14, and the 2nd leading cause of death in Indian teenagers and young adults age 15 to 24. In addition, the IHS data indicate that Indian teenagers/young adults' suicide rate is 2.5 times greater than the nationwide U.S. rate. Young Indian men are more at risk to completed suicides, whereas young Indian women are more at risk to suicide ideation or thoughts.

Many Are at Early Risk

In addition, data from the biennial BIA [Bureau of Indian Affairs] High School and Middle School Youth Risk Behavior Surveys (YRBS) provide insight into the progression Indian children and teens go through from feeling sad or hopeless, to seriously considering suicide, to making a suicide plan, to actually attempting suicide, to incurring serious injury requiring treatment by a medical professional. The data demonstrate that approximately one-third of Indian children and teens feel sad or hopeless, in a given year, which is an early stage in a suicidal event. The most recent BIA YRBS data for Indian students enrolled in 2003 show that for Indian high school students:

- 21% seriously considered attempting suicide in the last year [2005], and
- 18% actually attempted suicide one or more times in the last year.

For Indian middle school students, the data show that:

- 26% seriously considered attempting suicide, at some time in their life, and
- 15% had attempted suicide.

Furthermore, statistics from the 2002 Annual Report of the Alaska Bureau of Vital Statistics show that between 1990 and 1999, Alaska Native teens committed suicide at a rate of 110 per 100,000 or over five times greater than the rate of 20 per 100,000 non-Native teenagers in Alaska.

Twenty-one percent of Indian high school students say they have seriously considered suicide, and 18 percent have actually attempted suicide.

Although national hard data are not available on Indian country residents, the professional literature strongly suggests a close association between parental alcohol and drug abuse, child abuse (whether emotional, physical or sexual), domestic violence and suicide in children and teens. Often suicide may be the only way a child or teen sees of extricating him/herself from a hostile or threatening environment. However, the following can help prevent suicide in Indian Country:

- improved housing conditions
- increased prevention and treatment services
- increased identification of at-risk individuals and families and referral to services
- enhanced community development and capacity building through technical assistance and training for tribal leaders and staff

BIA programs assist tribal communities to develop their natural and social-economic infrastructures (i.e., tribal governments, tribal courts, cultural vitalization, community capabilities, etc.) or provide services to fill infrastructure gaps (i.e., education, law enforcement, social services, housing improvement, transportation and so on). For the BIA, suicidal events significantly impact law enforcement personnel since they are the most likely first responders and have a significant impact on BIA/tribal school teachers and students when the suicidal individual is a child or teenager.

Coordinated Efforts Can Improve Students' Safety

BIA's Law Enforcement, Education and Tribal Services programs continually seek ways to collaborate and to support activities directed at suicide prevention and services coordination. An example of this type of coordination is the BIA Rocky Mountain Region (Montana and Wyoming) Native American Youth Suicide Prevention Health Initiative developed and presented by BIA, IHS and Indian Development and Education Alliance (IDEA). The region also hosted a workshop on Native American Youth Suicide Prevention Training of Trainers in 2005, which included "natural healers" to provide referral and support.

Within the BIA's OIEP [Office of Indian Education Programs] school system all Bureau-funded schools receive supplemental program funds, through the US Department of Education, to operate a Safe and Drug-free School program. Schools use these funds to address a myriad of issues to make their schools safe places for students and staff. BIA schools receive about $92 per student enrolled and use these funds to address a myriad of issues to make their schools safe places for students and staff. Past initiatives included the Comprehensive School Health Program where OIEP partnered with IHS and the National Centers for Disease Control [and Prevention] to assist schools in developing plans that brought together the involvement of their community partners such as local law enforcement, social services, and mental and physical health providers.

OIEP is committed to ensuring a safe and secure environment for our students. Our focus is the implementation of suicide prevention strategies. The OIEP's Center of School Improvement launched a Suicide Prevention Initiative using the IHS endorsed

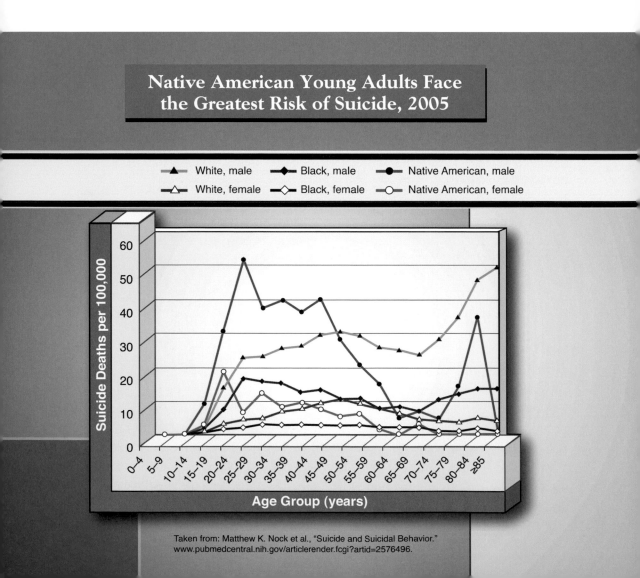

Native American Young Adults Face the Greatest Risk of Suicide, 2005

Taken from: Matthew K. Nock et al., "Suicide and Suicidal Behavior." www.pubmedcentral.nih.gov/articlerender.fcgi?artid=2576496.

scientifically researched based Question Persuade Respond (QPR) model. QPR is an aggressive intervention program focused on suicide prevention. An initial training in QPR was held in Denver, Colorado in August of 2004 and provided training on the QPR model to all 184 BIA funded schools and dormitories. Administrators at the school and dorm level were instructed to complete 100% training in the QPR suicide prevention model for staff at their respective schools. Additional sets of training material have been distributed to the schools and dorms through the Education Line Offices on an annual basis. In 2004, OIEP provided training opportunities for schools to establish crisis intervention teams to address potential suicide incidents, using the QPR model.

OIEP has provided training almost yearly on prevention of risky behaviors as well as preparation required to address almost any emergency situation. Most recently OIEP sponsored a nationwide event whereby students were dismissed for the afternoon while staff met to review their policies and procedures addressing emergency situations. [In May 2006], the majority of Bureau-funded schools attended a two-day "Safe Schools" training in Denver, Colorado. The focus of the training was on emergency preparedness for any type of emergency situation that would include what to do in an attempted suicide or suicide incident.

Working Together to Prevent Future Suicide Attempts

In summary, the BIA, IHS, Substance Abuse and Mental Health Services Administration, other Federal agencies, and Indian tribes must continue to work together to address all aspects of suicidal events—both before and after the event happens. Because most Indian programs fall within the respective missions of the BIA or the IHS, it is essential that the programs, in each respective agency, that directly or indirectly relate to suicidal events are coordinated and function collaboratively. BIA invites other Federal, state and tribal organizations and agencies to contact BIA regarding programmatic information, to coordinate efforts and resources, and to collaborate in addressing suicidal Indian children, teens and young adults.

FOUR

Young, Unmarried Soldiers Are at Greater Risk for Suicide

Paul J. Fink

> Paul J. Fink is a psychiatrist, a consultant, and a professor of psychiatry at Temple University in Pennsylvania. In this article he examines many of the possible explanations for the high rate of suicide among young, unmarried U.S. soldiers. Some of the possibilities Fink explores include multiple redeployments, survivor guilt, the realities of home life upon return, war guilt, mental illness, and the availability of firearms.

When the Army released its report, newspapers across the country (and perhaps around the world) ran headlines like this: "More U.S. Soldiers Committed Suicide in 2007 Than at Any Time Since the First Gulf War." For those of us who tend to the mental health of others, these suicides are particularly tragic.

We are sending young people to war at a time in their lives when, developmentally, they want to be autonomous. The majority of these young people—most of whom are men—have never witnessed death before, certainly not to the extent that they see it while in combat.

We can only speculate about the underlying reasons for their decisions to take their lives. One factor could be the extended

Paul J. Fink, "Fink! Still at Large: A Recent Report on Suicide in the U.S. Army Shows That Suicidal Behaviors Are More Common Among Young, Unmarried Soldiers. What Factors Might Make Young People More Vulnerable?" *Clinical Psychiatry News*, vol. 36, July 2008, p. 21. Copyright © 2008 International Medical News Group. Reproduced by permission.

amount of time in which they are deployed. Our volunteer Army needs manpower, and we do not have a plethora of men and women waiting in the wings to fight. One major supposition about the suicides is that they could be related to these redeployments. The Army's data show that 7% of the soldiers who either had completed or attempted suicide [in 2007] had a history of multiple deployments to Iraq or Afghanistan. It must be very disheartening to wait for the day when you expect to be sent home to your family—and then find out that you have to return to active duty in a month.

These young men are dispatched to a land that is foreign and hostile. The justifications for the war have been ambiguous at best, and this probably has made it difficult for some soldiers—particularly the younger ones—to develop the kind of patriotism that their grandfathers had during World War II.

When today's soldiers arrive in the theater, many see their buddies get killed, and they have no recourse—other than to get angry or to get out. And this desire to get out can lead to suicide. After all, a soldier cannot just announce to his sergeant that he is leaving.

So, one of the causes of suicide might be survivor guilt. This phenomenon has been written about extensively and was eloquently portrayed by Rod Steiger in *The Pawnbroker*, a powerful 1965 film about the inner life of a Jewish pawnbroker and concentration camp survivor. When someone you care for dies, the question often becomes: Why him and not me? Certainly, the pain prompting such a question is palpable in the armed services, where the soldier has spent months in close quarters with, and often developed close emotional ties to, his comrades.

Problems at Home

The Army has developed an exquisite data system—the Army Suicide Event Report (ASER)—aimed at recording suicidal events. In the report, the Army has been very careful to record whether the suicide occurred during the soldier's deployment or after the return home. For many, the realities of their lives at

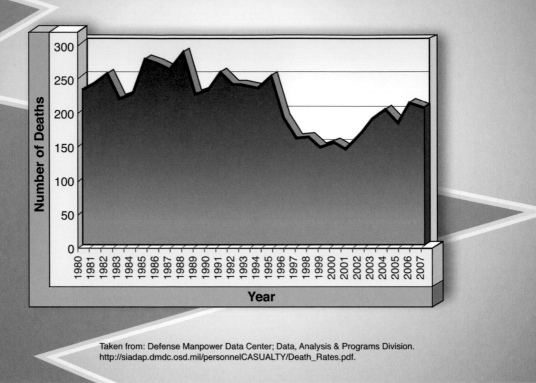

Suicides Among Soldiers on Active Duty

Taken from: Defense Manpower Data Center; Data, Analysis & Programs Division.
http://siadap.dmdc.osd.mil/personnelCASUALTY/Death_Rates.pdf.

home might have been drab, compared with the constant state of tension and excitement of war. Life events such as broken love affairs, unhappy marriages, and other issues on the home front can overwhelm and depress anyone.

We know that depression is almost always a factor in suicide, as it was with these young people. Although the Army lists depression as making up only 10% of the motivators, it also lists depressive symptoms such as hopelessness (11%), emotional relief (11%) and avoidance or escape (8%), so one could conclude that a large number of those soldiers were depressed when they took their lives.

The record shows that 30% of the suicide victims had used alcohol or drugs during the event. When they eliminated the responders who listed "I don't know," the percentage went up to 46. A significant number had told people of their intent to take their lives, and that should have been enough to alert coworkers and families of real danger. We must help people become more responsive to the potential of suicide.

The psychiatric literature on suicide both in adults and children is robust. Many young soldiers are still children in many ways. About 40% of those who died had been separated or were having relationship issues at the time of the suicide.

We are cognizant that people who commit suicide often are impulsive and see no other way out of their psychological pain. Often, that pain is guilt. I have already mentioned survivor guilt. But war gives people many opportunities to feel guilty: They are involved with killing unarmed or innocent civilians, they have contributed to the death of a colleague, their hatred for an officer or fellow soldier is very high, or their hatred for war makes them feel unpatriotic, "unAmerican," or just bad for being in the wrong place at the wrong time.

Psychological Pain and Hopelessness

Discouragement often leads soldiers to feel hopeless with no sense of the future of their own ambitions once they get out. If this person has a deep sense that he or she is going to die, pushing things along might not seem very frightening.

Most people I have interviewed who have made a serious attempt to die see no reason to go on. Life is meaningless to them. In recent years, I have noticed that most of these suicidal people have histories of enormous abuse, having been repeatedly trained to believe that they are worthless.

The statistics on existing mental illness in both completions and attempts is significant in the ASER. Among those who successfully killed themselves, 24% had been diagnosed with a mood disorder and 20% had been diagnosed with an anxiety disorder. In the latter group, 7% had posttraumatic stress disorder (PTSD) and 18% had a history of substance abuse.

It is interesting to note that "combat fatigue" was used as a diagnosis during World War II to patch the guy up and send him back into battle. Combat fatigue was the precursor of PTSD, and perhaps the Army is doing the same thing for young people who develop PTSD while deployed. Those in charge of the war and in need of troops seem to have little regard for individual men and women, and instead keep their eyes on the target—which is fighting the war.

Whether or not a suicide occurs depends on a great deal of emotional vulnerability, and throughout this [viewpoint], I have been referring to varying levels of vulnerability in some men and women who kill themselves. Even such a "minor" factor as the presence and availability of guns needs to be considered. According to ASER, "firearms were the most common method of completed suicide, and overdoses and cutting were the most common methods of self-harm not resulting in death."

Reluctance to Seek Help

In addition, there is the sense of humiliation that some soldiers might feel when someone suggests a visit to a professional. The seeking out of professional help might result in the soldier's losing a great deal of status and stature among his comrades and superiors. A person who is supposed to be a "man," a "fighter," a "protector of his country," should not be seen as having a mental illness or emotional disturbance.

If he becomes depressed during his tour of duty, his efforts not to reveal his ambivalence, sadness, tears, or other signs of the illness might increase his stress level to the point where he is driven to thoughts of suicide or action.

Other important vulnerabilities include prior mental problems, low self-esteem, and an inability to take the kind of criticism and pressures that sergeants are reputed to provide.

In addition, mental problems or other issues in the soldier's home life might be major contributors to the development of depressive symptoms and, ultimately, to suicide.

This has become such important sequelae [aftereffects] of war, because it's sad enough that we take young people out of the normal course of their lives and send them to hostile foreign territory to risk their lives. When the soldier takes his own life, it is often incomprehensible to civilians, because few people in the country stop to think about the kinds of stressors that would lead a soldier to kill himself.

Exposure to Death

In the ASER report, there is a category related to the soldiers' experiences in direct combat—such as seeing casualties, being injured, witnessing killing, seeing dead bodies, and having killed others—which might be very disturbing to the young person. Even if they know that "war is hell," such experiences can be devastating to a sensitive "kid" whose life experience might not even include the loss of a grandparent.

No one knows how these events are processed in the mind. I've discussed a few ways these issues might be handled by the soldier, including survivor guilt and depression. But in truth, we don't know, and in the Army, this is the way war goes. There is no way to determine by looking at a person how he is feeling. I certainly wish we could!

All of the usual indicators of lethality must be applied to these young men. For example, 10% of those in the 2007 ASER report had a family member who had completed a suicide. We don't know how many of them had tried suicide before, but we must pay more attention to factors that might indicate danger.

The abuse history of the completers and attempters is also interesting. Many had been victims of physical and/or sexual abuse as children. Other important historical information includes excessive debt or bankruptcy (9%), job problems (22%), and poor performance evaluations (9%).

Unknown and Unpredictable Suicide Cases

All of us who are involved with delinquent and criminal systems know of cases of "suicide by cop." This occurs when a person points a gun at a police officer, who then shoots him. After the death of the victim, it is discovered that the gun was not loaded. In some cases, no gun was ever found.

Many soldiers returning from Iraq and Afghanistan suffer from post-traumatic stress disorder (PTSD), which makes them susceptible to depression and attempting suicide.

We will never know how many heroes in Iraq and Afghanistan put themselves in the line of fire purposely to die bravely instead of putting an end to their own lives. This is one of the great unknowns in the area of soldier suicides.

For young people who oppose the war and find themselves killing others, it might be too overwhelming, and they might find that this method is easier and more socially acceptable than suicide.

We are involved in a terrible war, and we can only hope that it will be over soon. In the meantime, each week 5–10 American soldiers die exclusive of suicide. We as a nation must grieve for these destroyed lives and families.

In addition to more than 4,000 dead soldiers, there are 30,000 seriously wounded young people, and that [figure] does not include thousands of kids who come home with severe PTSD.

The high suicide rate is truly a disgrace. We should try to figure out how to screen young people before they are taken into the armed forces and undergo the horrors of war.

According to the Army Suicide Event Report for 2007, 24% of those who successfully killed themselves had been diagnosed with a mood disorder.

FIVE

The Desire for Attention Motivates Teens to Commit Suicide

Kathy Brewis

Kathy Brewis, currently a commissioning editor, has been with the British weekly newsmagazine *Sunday Times* for ten years. In this article, written in late January 2008, she examines possible causes behind a cluster of seven suicides committed in or near a small mining town in Wales. By late February 2008, newspapers reported as many as seventeen total suicides, and by November 2008 the total had reached twenty-three over a two-year period.

Suicide is far from painless, both for the people who do it and for the ones they leave behind. The cluster of seven suicides in Bridgend, south Wales, has left scores of grieving relatives and friends and the rest of us stunned at the thought that these young people—some pictured partying just days earlier—could take their own lives.

Disturbingly, the town's teenage population seem less surprised by the tragic events. Below a steady drizzle, a group of teenagers outside a Bridgend off-licence [liquor store] discuss their dead friend Natasha Randall, the most recent in the series of suicides to have afflicted the town and the only girl. Their rationale is shocking.

Hopelessness in Bridgend

"Perhaps she just got bored," says Aaron, a 17-year-old in a hooded top and trainers. "It's depressing living here. There's nothing to do and we'll never get decent jobs. The best I can hope for is to carry on stacking shelves at Tesco."

Already two other teenagers have tried to end their lives and 12 pupils at a comprehensive school are on suicide watch. Danielle, a 16-year-old in a white tracksuit, says: "Kids round here have been drinking, smoking dope, taking ecstasy and having sex since they were 13 or 14. By the time they reach my age they've done everything. The combination of booze, drugs and the boredom of living around here screws young people up so much that they think killing themselves will be exciting."

"We know young people can get things out of proportion," says Anne Parry, chairwoman of the charity Papyrus which aims to prevent teenage suicide. "They feel things more passionately and they are more impulsive and that can be dangerous. They don't always associate suicide with being dead for ever." Papyrus is run by people who have lost children to suicide, who know first-hand the devastation that it brings.

"Suicide is always shocking," says Parry. "But it is a fact of life. It's no good thinking this won't happen in your family. Sadly, it does. No family is immune. As a society we have to ask ourselves: is there enough support around this young person? What can we all do to stop this?"

What makes a teenager turn to suicide? There are no easy answers and cases vary—one youngster might kill himself apparently out of the blue while another talks about it obsessively for months beforehand. But there are common factors.

"A suicidal teenager feels hopeless. They often feel no one cares about them, perhaps even that it would be better for everybody if they weren't there. If a young person is feeling suicidal they must confront that head-on and seek help."

The Internet Encourages Dangerous Networking

If the right sort of help is not on hand, teenagers might be encouraged further towards despair and death. There are numerous internet

Officials in Bridgend, Wales, meet with the press to discuss the rash of teen suicides occurring in their community.

sites where youngsters discuss methods and attempts at suicide—which are now to be part of a government review of safety on the web—to be met with comments like: "You want to be dead but ur just scared of the process that gets u there. It's normal."

Even the general social networking sites like Bebo—which millions of British teenagers use—can play a part.

Three of the Bridgend suicides—Zachary Barnes, Liam Clarke and Natasha Randall—all shared friends on Bebo. Randall posted a message to Liam following his death whose almost jokey tone reflects the slight unreality that often attaches to online behaviour: "RIP Clarky boy!! gonna miss ya! allways remember the good times! love ya x". Randall's site—perhaps typical of many teenagers' featured sex quizzes and pictures of herself in revealing outfits.

Online "memorials," eerily reminiscent of the flowers and cards left at roadside accident sites by friends and strangers alike, are now commonplace. Randall's suicide attracted hundreds of comments before her profile was taken down . . . most of which made reference to her looks and praised her. Even the negative comments alluded to the attention she was receiving after her death.

"Chrissie" wrote: "R.I.P Like . . . But why? . . . Isit Tru She Wanted More Bebo Views? Hope Your Lookin Down On Your Family & Friends. They Must Be In Peices Because Of Youu . . . No Need Too Do Somethin Soo Selfish."

Suicide Clusters

It's too simple to blame the internet for a phenomenon that, according to Loren Coleman, author of the book *Suicide Clusters*, has ebbed and flowed throughout the centuries and is often linked to complex social factors. In the depression of the 1930s, he points out, Americans blamed comic books for suicides plainly linked to economic deprivation. Today, says Coleman, "it's not video games, it's not the media, it's not television. It's part of the human condition."

It's nothing new, he claims: "Sigmund Freud held a conference on youth suicide clusters in the 1920s." When Coleman published his book in 1987, nobody believed they were a phenomenon. Now, he says, it's a no-brainer. "The particulars are a small geographical area, similar ages and backgrounds and similar method. All these kids died by hanging. That's a method that takes some thought and it's very painful. It's almost certainly because they heard about it and chose it in a deliberate fashion.

"People find it easier to accept the idea in families, like the Hemingway family, where five people chose suicide. Well, these youths are like an extended family.

"If you're vulnerable and desperate, you're easily affected by models. You think: if they figured suicide was their option, maybe I should."

It is an unpalatable but undeniable fact that death attracts attention. "Reality TV means young people are constantly bombarded with instant fame and instant success. A young person in a deprived area sees this and it's psychologically destructive. They think: if I'm a nobody but I commit suicide, I'll be a somebody. I'll get my photo in the papers, I'll have a memorial on the internet. How can I be a celebrity? Well, if I don't get onto Big Brother, an alternative is death. My friends are doing it."

A Unique Approach

Dr Arthur Cassidy, the social psychologist, set up a mobile suicide prevention unit in Co Armagh [Northern Ireland] after a suicide cluster in the area claimed three boys in the space of a month last summer [2007]. He takes his converted caravan to where young people gather and he and his team make themselves available to the alienated young people who feel trapped with no future beyond their immediate grim surroundings.

"They don't see Samaritans posters or they feel that that's for adults," he explains. "So we go to them. When their minds are in that sort of turmoil they need to talk about it in confidence. We try to break down the negative thought patterns in which death is an option and replace them with a learned optimism."

Teenagers are trying out different identities, looking for role models, he adds.

So they are easily influenced by self-harming celebrities in the tabloid newspapers and stories of suicide: "The media can romanticise death. There are music and films which glorify suicide. A heavy-metaller who writes suicidal lyrics can appeal to them; their own negative self-concept is consistent with what they read about these musicians who have negative life experiences, are addicted to drugs and so on."

There used to be five youth focus groups in Bridgend, where teenagers could turn for counselling, but funding was withdrawn and now there is only one. "Bridgend has poverty, unemployment, it's an old mining town . . . the osmosis of depression, the groundlessness, has leaked through to the youth. What is there for young people if they stay in that community? What sense of hope has been lost?" says Coleman.

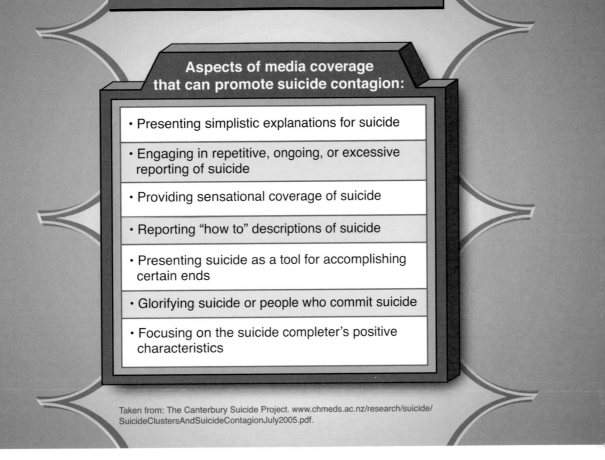

"People forget that suicide is about pain. It's about escaping from pain, not ending your life. So the only way we can help young people is to talk to them about that pain. And it's up to us to say that yes, there are some bad parts of life that we all go through, but life is really pretty wonderful."

SIX

Antidepressants Contribute to an Increase in Teen Suicides

Kirsten Weir

> Kirsten Weir, a freelance journalist specializing in stories about science, health, and the environment, writes here for *Current Health 2*, a publication used in middle and high school classrooms. In this article she discusses reported links between antidepressant drugs and teen suicides, addressing tragic cases, known risks, and Federal Drug Administration (FDA) actions.

On April 20, 1999, Mark Taylor was caught in the shooting spree that erupted at the Columbine High School in Littleton, Colorado. Classmate Eric Harris shot Taylor twice in the back and five times in the chest.

Today, Taylor, who still has a bullet lodged near his heart, often speaks to civic groups across the country. His topic: the dangers of antidepressant drugs. Eric Harris was taking a prescription antidepressant drug when, along with fellow student Dylan Klebold, he killed 12 classmates and a teacher, injured more than 20 others, and then killed himself.

[In 2004], Taylor testified at a U.S. Food and Drug Administration (FDA) hearing held to address concerns about reports of suicidal ideas and behavior among children and adolescents taking antidepressant medications. "Do you people have children? Do you? Do any of you? Have any of you had anyone that has died on these drugs?" Taylor asked. "This is a shame, and it ought to be stopped today, not next week."

A New Warning

Depression is a psychiatric disorder marked by an inability to concentrate; a loss of appetite; insomnia (inability to sleep) or oversleeping; and feelings of extreme sadness, guilt, and hopelessness. It can affect anyone of any age. Depression affects up to 2.5 percent of children and about 8 percent of adolescents in the United States, according to the National Institute of Mental Health.

A number of drugs are prescribed to treat depression, but many people, Mark Taylor among them, are particularly concerned about selective serotonin reuptake inhibitors (SSRIs). Drugs of this type, including Prozac, Paxil, Luvox, and Zoloft, are commonly prescribed for depression.

Almost all SSRIs have been approved only for adults. Nevertheless, doctors often prescribe them for children and teens. According to the Agency for Healthcare Research and Quality, the number of SSRI prescriptions for patients under age 20 increased 62 percent between 1995 and 1999.

Side effects of SSRIs range from nausea and high blood pressure to agitation and sleep disorders. Drug companies also admit that in rare cases SSRIs can cause psychotic, violent, or suicidal feelings. Ann Blake Tracy, executive director of the International Coalition for Drug Awareness, also testified at the FDA hearing. "I am greatly concerned about the use of these drugs among children, with developing brains, who have far more reactions than the general public would," she said.

The October 2004 Federal Drug Administration (FDA) Black Box Warning

In 2004, the FDA directed drug manufacturers to add a "black box" warning to the health professional labeling of all antidepressant medications. The label was to warn the public about the increased risk of suicidal thoughts and behavior (suicidality) in children and adolescents being treated with antidepressant medications.

Antidepressants increase the risk of suicidal thinking and behavior (suicidality) in children and adolescents with major depressive disorder (MDD) and other psychiatric disorders. Anyone considering the use of [Drug Name] or any other antidepressant in a child or adolescent must balance this risk with the clinical need. Patients who are started on therapy should be observed closely for clinical worsening, suicidality, or unusual changes in behavior. Families and care-givers should be advised of the need for close observation and communication with the prescriber. [Drug Name] is not approved for use in pediatric patients except for patients with [Any approved pediatric claims here]. (See Warnings and Precautions: Pediatric Use).

Pooled analyses of short-term (four to sixteen weeks) placebo-controlled trials of nine antidepressant drugs (SSRIs and others) in children and adolescents with MDD, obsessive compulsive disorder (OCD), or other psychiatric disorders (a total of 24 trials involving over 4400 patients) have revealed a greater risk of adverse events representing suicidal thinking or behavior (suicidality) during the first few months of treatment in those receiving antidepressants. The average risk of such events on drug was 4 percent, twice the placebo risk of 2 percent. No suicides occurred in these trials.

Taken from: U.S. Food and Drug Administration Labeling Change Request Letter for Antidepressant Medications. www.fda.gov/Drugs/DrugSafety/InformationbyDrugClass/ucm096352.htm.

Scientific Evidence Is Against Antidepressants

Last year's [2004] FDA hearing was prompted by a report suggesting that children who took Paxil had a higher risk of suicidal thoughts and actions compared with those given a placebo. A placebo is a substance containing no medication that is given as a test to determine how effective medically active drugs are.

In December 2003, British health authorities banned new prescriptions of all SSRIs except Prozac for children under 18. That decision was based on a review by medical experts, who found that the risks of taking the drugs outweighed the benefits.

Last year, the FDA commissioned its own large study, which combined the results of 24 smaller studies involving more than 4,400 children and teenagers who took either placebos or antidepressants for one to four months. The researchers looked at nine antidepressant drugs, including SSRIs. Although none of the teens in the study committed suicide, some young patients became suicidal. On placebos, two of every 100 kids became suicidal. On the antidepressants, twice as many, or four of every 100 young patients, became suicidal.

In October 2004, the FDA directed manufacturers to add a "black box" warning to the labels of all antidepressant medications to alert health-care providers to an increased risk of suicidality (suicidal thinking and behavior) in children and adolescents who are treated with these drugs. The black box warning is the most serious warning used in the labeling of prescription medications.

The FDA has also required drug manufacturers to note the approved uses of these drugs in children and adolescents. Currently, Prozac is the only medication approved to treat depression in patients under 18.

The new warning language does not ban the use of antidepressants in children and adolescents. The FDA recognizes that depression can have serious consequences. The action simply warns of the risks of the drugs and encourages physicians to balance risk with need.

The Drugs' Dangerous Side Effects

Researchers aren't entirely sure why SSRIs might cause violence or suicide. One theory focuses on akathisia, a severe form of restlessness that can be a side effect of the drugs, especially in the first few weeks as the body adjusts to the new medication. Supporters of this theory say that extreme agitation pushes some patients over the edge.

After the Columbine incident, four psychiatrists investigated the shooting and concluded that Eric Harris had suffered from manic psychosis, an extremely excited mental state in which a person's perception of reality is impaired. Harris had been taking the drug Luvox. According to Blake Tracy, "All you have to do is read the Luvox package insert to see that Eric's actions were due to an adverse reaction to this drug," she said. Mark Taylor filed a lawsuit against Solvay Pharmaceuticals, the maker of the drug. The suit was settled when the company agreed to donate $10,000 to the American Cancer Society.

Prozac is one of a number of antidepressants used to treat depression in U.S. children and adolescents. Some studies show that taking such medication can increase suicidality in teens and children.

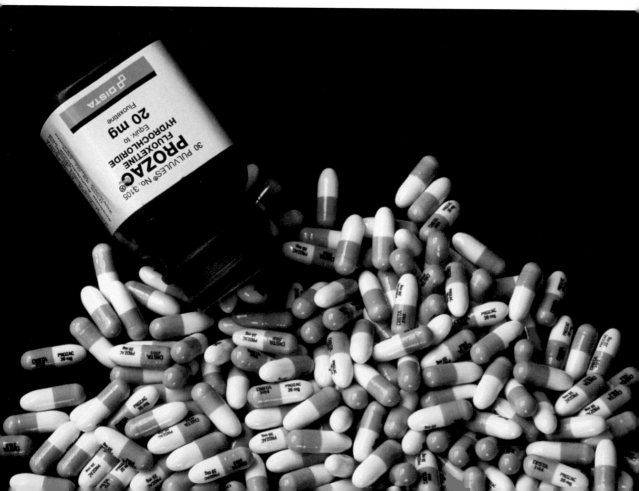

Supporters of SSRIs argue that in cases of suicide, the drugs have done more good than harm—they have prevented more suicides than they've caused. According to the Centers for Disease Control and Prevention, suicide is the third leading cause of death among 15- to 24-year-olds. Because depressed patients are already at an increased risk of suicide, researchers have difficulty determining whether suicidal behavior is caused by depression or by the drugs intended to treat it.

"There is a suggestion that about 3 percent of [SSRI users] may have a worsening of behavior," said Graham Emslie, a psychiatrist at the University of Texas Southwestern Medical Center. "However, the evidence is stronger that 50 to 60 percent of people have relief of depression, and most with suicidal thoughts will improve."

No one is sure how to predict which patients will experience suicidal thoughts or manic psychosis while taking SSRIs. Because of that, many doctors say, patients should be monitored closely for the first few weeks they take the drugs. Children and teens should be watched for negative responses, such as the jittery behavior associated with akathisia.

Anyone who has been prescribed SSRIs shouldn't stop taking them suddenly, say doctors. Sometimes severe physical or psychological side effects can occur. Patients who wish to stop taking the drugs should consult with a doctor to taper off gradually.

SEVEN

The Absence of Prescribed Antidepressants Has Increased the Rate of Teen Suicides

Adverse Event Reporting News

Adverse Event Reporting News covers adverse medical events, including drug reactions, medical device reports, vaccine reactions, and dietary supplement reactions, for subscribers in the health care industry. This article is an overview of several studies that report correlations between decreased use of antidepressants and an increased risk of suicide in young people. The studies were conducted after opposing studies were released that found a correlation between antidepressant use and suicide in teens, which resulted in strong warning labels on these medications and consequently a decrease in prescribing them for teens.

Warnings from federal regulators four years ago [in 2003] that antidepressants were increasing the risk of suicidal behavior among young people led to a precipitous drop in the use of the drugs. Now new studies have found that the drop coincides

"Youth Suicides Increased as Antidepressant Use Fell," Adverse Event Reporting News, vol. 4, September 10, 2007, pp. 7–8. Reproduced by permission of Washington Information Source Co., Leesburg, VA.

with an unprecedented increase in the number of suicides among children.

A study published in the September issue of the *American Journal of Psychiatry* (AJP) found that from 2003 to 2004, the suicide rate among Americans younger than 19 rose 14%, the most dramatic one-year change since the government started collecting suicide statistics in 1979, *The Washington Post* reported Sept. 6 [2007].

The following day, the Centers for Disease Control [and Prevention] (CDC) reported that the rate of suicide in Americans ages 10 to 24 increased 8% from 2003 to 2004, the largest jump in more than 15 years.

A Possible Cause

Some psychiatrists argue that the reason for the increase is the decline in prescriptions of antidepressant drugs like Prozac to young people since 2003, leaving more cases of serious depression untreated. Others say that it is impossible to know if the increase is linked to patterns of antidepressant prescriptions. The one-year spike in suicides could be a statistical fluctuation, they say, and not the start of a trend.

The increase was particularly sharp among adolescents, especially, CDC stated.

The data from the study in the *AJP* suggest that for every 20% decline in antidepressant use among patients of all ages in the United States, an additional 3,040 suicides per year would occur, said Robert Gibbons, a professor of biostatistics and psychiatry at the University of Illinois at Chicago, who did the study. About 32,000 Americans commit suicide each year.

CDC's analysis found that in 2004 there were 4,599 suicides in Americans ages 10 to 24, up from 4,232 in 2003, for a rate of 7.32 per 100,000 people that age. In the years before that, the rate had dropped to 6.78 per 100,000 in 2003 from 9.48 per 100,000 in 1990.

Thomas Insel, M.D., director of the National Institute of Mental Health [NIMH] told *The Post*, "We may have inadvertently created a problem by putting a black box warning on medications that were useful." He added, "If the drugs were doing more harm than good, then the reduction in prescription rates should mean

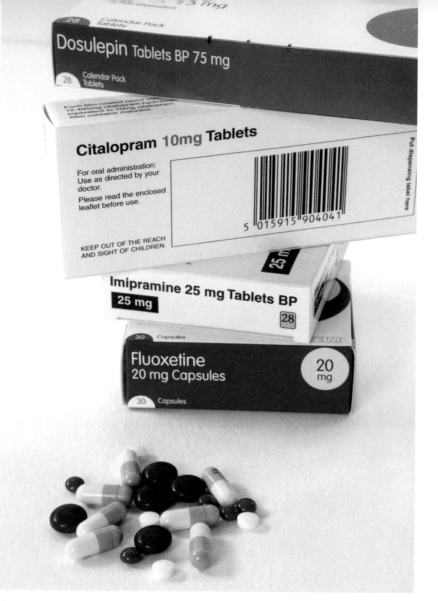

In 2003, studies found that giving teens antidepressants increased the risk of suicide, leading to a drop in prescribing such drugs. But new research indicates that the teen suicide rate actually went up when doctors prescribed fewer antidepressants.

the risk of suicide should go way down, and it hasn't gone down at all—it has gone up."

However, Thomas Laughren, M.D., director of the division of psychiatry products at FDA [Food and Drug Administration], said in a conference call with reporters that the agency would need to see more data over time, linking declines in prescriptions to suicide risk before revisiting any of its decisions.

"You simply cannot reach causal conclusions" from the new CDC data, Laughren said.

A Strong Controversy

These new findings are the latest developments in a controversy marked by complex science and passionate advocates. In 2003 and 2004, FDA issued a series of warnings that clinical trials had detected an increase in suicidal thinking among children and adolescents taking a class of antidepressants known as selective serotonin reuptake inhibitors (SSRIs), compared with children and adolescents given sugar pills. In late 2004, the agency called for a "black box" warning on the drugs to call attention to the potential risk, and expanded it last December [2006] to include young adults.

The warnings led to a broad decline in SSRI prescriptions for all patients younger than 60, Gibbons said. Prescription rates continued to rise among those older than 60, and this was the only group in which suicides dropped between 2003 and 2004, his study found.

The study included the Netherlands, which had a 22% decrease in antidepressant use among children between 2003 and 2005. The suicide rate among youngsters there increased by 49% in that period.

The trend lines do not prove that suicides rose because of the drop in prescriptions, but Gibbons, Insel and other experts said the international evidence leaves few other plausible explanations. Previous studies have shown that U.S. suicide rates are lower in counties where antidepressant use is higher, and a recent study of 200,000 depressed veterans found that those taking an antidepressant had one-third the risk of suicide of those who were not.

David Healy, a British psychiatrist who has been critical of the drugs, disagrees. He said that the increase in suicides was more likely caused by the growing use of antipsychotic drugs among

Suicide Rates of Youth by Age Group, Sex, and Year, 1990–2004

Suicide rates per 100,000 in sex/age group:			
Year	Females Aged 10–14	Females Aged 15–19	Males Aged 10–14	Males Aged 15–19
1990	0.8	3.73	2.17	18.17
1991	0.67	3.7	2.28	17.92
1992	0.9	3.42	2.4	17.61
1993	0.93	3.8	2.4	17.39
1994	0.95	3.44	2.36	17.95
1995	0.82	3.07	2.57	17.11
1996	0.8	3.49	2.23	15.38
1997	0.76	3.31	2.29	14.94
1998	0.86	2.84	2.3	14.34
1999	0.51	2.75	1.85	13.05
2000	0.62	2.75	2.26	13
2001	0.64	2.7	1.93	12.87
2002	0.62	2.36	1.81	12.22
2003	0.54	2.66	1.73	11.61
2004	0.95	3.52	1.71	12.65

Taken from: Centers for Disease Control and Prevention, "Suicide Trends Among Youths and Young Adults Aged 10–24 Years—United States, 1990–2004," *Morbidity and Mortality Weekly Report*, vol. 56, no. 35, September 7, 2007. www.cdc.gov/mmwr/PDF/wk/mm5635.pdf.

children rather than a decline in antidepressant use. "I would be absolutely certain that the increase is not because kids are not being treated," he told *The Post*. "They may not be getting SSRIs, but they are getting psychotropics."

The *AJP* study was largely funded by the federal government. Pfizer, which makes Zoloft, provided some money for data collection, Gibbons said, but was not involved in the study and did not review the results before they were published.

More Monitoring Is Required

FDA required the warnings on the drugs' labels to prompt doctors to closely monitor patients they put on antidepressants, because of some evidence that the risk of suicide is highest shortly after treatment begins. Gibbons said that the decision was misguided and that the situation called for better education of physicians, not warnings.

Laughren told *The Post*, "FDA is obviously concerned about possible negative impacts of labeling changes but also feels a strong obligation to alert prescribers and patients to possible risks associated with the use of antidepressants." He added, "We will continue to monitor antidepressant use and suicide rates, and will take appropriate regulatory actions as new data become available."

NIMH's Insel said it is possible that antidepressants are lowering the risk of suicide overall, even as they increase the risk among a subset of patients. New research to be published soon examines genetic factors that may put some patients at particular risk, he added.

If regulators base their decisions on risks alone, he said, "you focus on that very tiny number of kids who may be at greater risk when they are treated and you ignore the very large benefit that might accrue to the other 99.9%."

Insel acknowledged that it may be a while before physicians have tests that can reliably predict which patents are likely to become suicidal as a result of the drugs. In the interim, he said, "if I had a child with depression, I would go after the best treatment but also provide the closest monitoring."

EIGHT

Cyberbullying Can Lead to Teen Suicide

Selena Roberts

Selena Roberts, a columnist for *The New York Times* sports department, writes here for *Sports Illustrated* magazine. She examines the problem of school bullying, particularly bullying by jocks and bullying online that ends in both murder and suicide. She also highlights an antibullying workshop that brings together all types of high school students and encourages them to look for solutions to the bullying problem.

"All the jocks stand up."

—Words allegedly uttered by Eric Harris and Dylan Klebold as they began a shooting rampage at Columbine (Colorado) High, leaving 15 dead, on April 20, 1999.

"Those motherf---- jocks."

—Passage in the online diary of Kimveer Gill, discovered after he opened fire at Dawson College in Montreal, killing one and injuring 19 before killing himself on September 13, 2006.

Jesus Salavar can spot the outcasts. They walk carefully enough not to bump anyone—not to draw any stares—as they try to slip through the low-slung hallways of Del Mar High in San Jose

[California]. There is a look the vulnerable possess: haunted. "You see the faces, and you see the expressions," says Salavar. "It makes you wonder, Is it happening to them?" Did they receive the text message about the hot girl who likes them only to find out it was a hoax? Did someone create a phony social networking profile of them that lists their turn-ons as Star Wars and animal porn?

Online Bullying Is Not Uncommon

The subjects of high-tech bullying are everywhere: In a Harris Interactive survey from March 2007, 43% of teens reported being targeted by online attacks. Salavar recognizes some of the victims.

A Harris interactive survey in 2007 found that 43 percent of teens reported being targeted by cyberbullies.

He looks for them, but not as a teacher, counselor or administrator. He is a 17-year-old student interested in political science. He is also an athlete—a jock, if you must—who played wide receiver and cornerback at Del Mar High [in 2007], proof a helmet doesn't necessarily obstruct a teenager's ability to look beyond himself. "I don't see [much bullying] at Del Mar, but in other places kids gets angry at [athletes] because they may say, 'Oh, you're a football player, you think you're better,'" Salavar says.

Michele Livingstone is a swimmer who is not self-immersed. She notices the nervous tics of the lonely during lunch at Branham High, located in the same Silicon Valley region as Del Mar. "You see them wandering around, going to their lockers six times at lunch," she says. "And they don't have to go to their lockers six times, but it's something to do. I feel for them."

Empathy isn't always a staple of the popular crowd, but the likable Livingstone, bubbly to the point of being carbonated, is turning 17 this week with the kind of perspective some adults don't possess. "Something simple—like saying hello—can change so much for someone who feels isolated," Livingstone says. "It's like they can say to themselves, O.K., not everyone hates me."

Working on Empathy

Along with Salavar and other athletes, Livingstone recently attended a three-hour antibullying workshop called Expect Respect, organized by Project Cornerstone, a Bay Area alliance developed after the Columbine massacre. Members of different school-age status groups are enlisted—from club leaders and prom queens to quarterbacks and wrestlers. The goal of the six-year-old program, which has extended to more than 300 San Jose–area schools, is to engage students in solutions. Be aware, be inclusive, be willing to alert someone if you sense that bullying has reached a crisis point.

Digital harassment can lead to tragedy. Last October [2006], after a cruel Internet ruse, 13-year-old Megan Meier of Dardenne Prairie, Missouri, hanged herself in her bedroom with a belt. "It's devastating for a lot of people," says Salavar, a Mexican immigrant who can remember being on the receiving end of racist slurs before he joined a football team at age 12. "The workshop made me even more aware. I watch for signs [in ways] I never did before."

The workshop dialogues aren't so much about squares and geeks but about kids who have no one, who can't find any label to fit but loner. They are often the targeted. "If it's a physical confrontation, you have a chance to fight back," Livingstone says. "It's the emotional stuff—the online stuff—that leaves the scars."

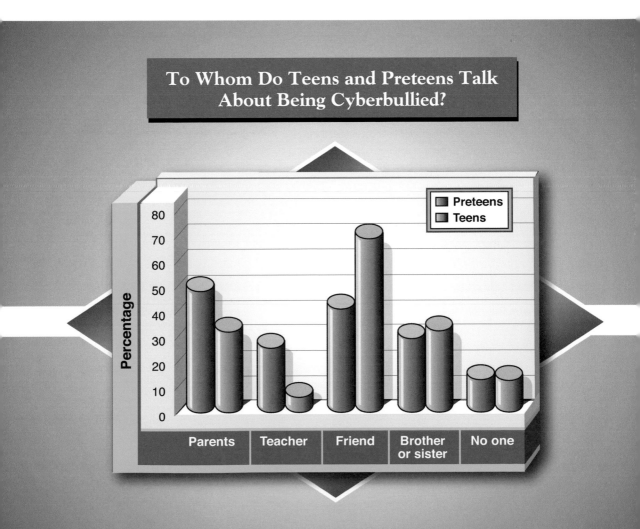

To Whom Do Teens and Preteens Talk About Being Cyberbullied?

Taken from: Opinion Research Corporation, Prepared for: Fight Crime: Invest in Kids, "Question D7: Have you told any of the following people about the mean, threatening, or hurtful messages you have received online?" *Cyber Bully Preteen Detailed Tabulations*, July 6, 2006. www.fightcrime.org/cyberbullying/cyberbullyingpreteen.pdf.

Are Jocks Really to Blame?

We've moved beyond stolen milk money to the Mean Girls who post slut lists on MySpace. And yet, the go-to bully of blame is still seen as the jock of movie lore—see *Heathers* or *Revenge of the Nerds*. Did catcalls of faggot and lipstick twins hurled by jocks at Columbine really push Klebold and Harris too far, or were the killers simply narcissists in trench coats? Did Gill, at Dawson, feel alienated by the glamorization of the jock culture, or did he seek an easy target for his rage? He posted this on Vampirefreaks.com: "Why does society applaud jocks. I don't understand. They are the worst kind of people on earth."

Though the hyperbole is agony being banged out on a keyboard, it is true that some tormentors do wear jerseys. At least in the hallways of Del Mar and Branham High, some athletes try to wear capes.

NINE

Silencing Cyberbullies Can Help Prevent Teen Suicides

Cindy Long

Cindy Long is a writer for *The NEA Today*, a publication of the National Education Association, the largest professional employee organization in the United States. Its members work at every level of education, from preschool to university graduate studies. In this article Long explains the unique cruelty of cyberbullying and cites some examples that have led to teen suicide. She challenges teachers to be aware and not to ignore evident bullying in their schools. She suggests addressing not necessarily the instigators, but the students who get swept up in the mob mentality that makes this kind of bullying so harmful.

Ryan Halligan was bullied so relentlessly at school he finally learned kickboxing to defend himself from the physical assaults. But when the attacks moved online, he had no way to fight back, and no refuge. Day and night, he received e-mails and instant messages from classmates ridiculing him and calling him a loser. When a pretty girl at school pretended to like him online but later revealed she was only joking, the taunting e-mails and instant messages increased, only with even more venom. A few

Teen Girls Experience Cyberbullying at Alarming Rates

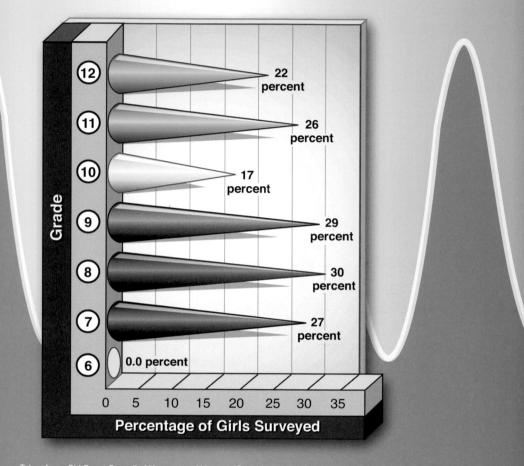

Taken from: Girl Scout Council of Vermont and Vermont Commission on Women, "What Teen Girls Say About Bullying and Harassment." www.women.state.vt.us/pdfs/What%20Girls%20Say%2007.pdf.

weeks later, in October 2003, Ryan hanged himself in his family's bathroom. He was 13 years old.

Now, Ryan's father travels to schools around the country to share the events that led up to his son's suicide and to warn educators and students about the dangers of cyberbullying. "Please don't ever forget Ryan's story," he says, "or the fragility of adolescence."

A New Kind of Bully

Cyberbullying is the use of electronic technology to deliberately harass or intimidate. Unlike the schoolyard bully of yesteryear, the cyberbully can hide behind online anonymity and attack around the clock, invading the privacy of a teen's home. With young people spending most of their free time online or texting their friends, digital bullies not only have ready access to victims, but also an audience—because without witnesses, virtual bullying loses its punch.

According to Pew Research, about one third (32 percent) of all teenagers who use the Internet say they have been targets of some form of cyberbullying that ranged from receiving threatening messages and having their private e-mails or text messages forwarded to having an embarrassing picture posted or rumors about them spread online.

Cyberbullying captured national attention [in 2006] when the story broke of 13-year-old Megan Meier, a Missouri girl who killed herself after an Internet hoax in which a fictitious "cute boy" was created by the mother and sister of Megan's classmate. The boy befriended Megan on the social networking site MySpace, but when he suddenly ganged up on her online with her friends, Megan crumbled, reminding everyone how vulnerable teenagers are to social pressure and how the agony of being singled out escalates with the wider forum provided by technology.

Even the slightest perceived misstep can be humiliating for an adolescent struggling with developing self-esteem, says Pennsylvania seventh-grade computer teacher Cathy Smith. But with the widespread use of technology, those missteps can be broadcast to the world.

"Instead of an incident being seen or heard by a few surrounding students, embarrassing moments can be caught on video or camera from a cell phone and be broadcast to the entire school, community, and across the nation," she says. "Imagine yourself as an awkward seventh-grader walking down the hallway when suddenly you're tripped. Maybe it's an accident, maybe not, but someone . . . gets a picture of you sprawled on the floor with your belongings thrown to the wind. . . . Now with camera phones, that moment can show up on YouTube for the entire world to see . . . and the victim gets humiliated over and over again every time someone new sees the incident."

As Ryan Halligan's and Megan Meier's parents can attest, cyberbullying incidents can be far more hurtful and humiliating than a video of someone tripping in the hallway. Even at Smith's middle school, some boys created an animation on a Web site where they virtually "beat up" one of their classmates on a regular basis and invited others to join them in the beatings. On another occasion, a "popular girl" placed her digital camera under a bathroom partition to capture an "unpopular" girl in a compromising position. In yet another incident, some of the middle school girls were pictured on a "Hot or Not" list that was e-mailed around to be voted on.

Why Teachers Should Pay Attention

Cyberbullying runs the gamut from minor incidents to major concerns, all of which should be addressed by educators, says Nancy Willard, executive director of the Center for Safe and Responsible Internet Use. "At the major concerns level, the students who are victimized can become very depressed. They're likely unable to study or focus in class and may avoid school, leading to school failure," she says. "Some are committing suicide. Some are engaging in school violence. Teachers must be concerned."

But what can educators do? "Talk about it," says Cathy Smith. "Define it and discuss expectations and consequences. Don't ignore it or take it lightly."

To get kids talking about cyberbullying, Smith meets her students where they live: online. She often shows them a video from the Ad Council where four middle school girls sit down together at school. After saying hello cheerfully, one looks over at her classmate and says matter-of-factly, "Megan, you're a tramp. Ryan Fitch told me you made out. Everyone knows. He says your breath smells like garbage. . . . You're the most desperate girl he knows, besides your mom. How many boyfriends does she have?" After several more cruel comments, the girl finally stops her insults, the screen goes black and a sentence appears: "If you wouldn't say it in person, why say it online?"

"This ad really got a reaction from the kids," Smith says. "They see how much farther kids will go and how cruel they'll get when they're able to type words in an e-mail or text and not have to say them face to face."

Smith also takes her kids to www.netsmartz.org where they download activity sheets and watch online videos. The "Real Stories" section has the most impact, Smith says, especially a video called *You Can't Take it Back* which plays on students' empathy and on an event that occurred at their school. It's narrated by a teenage boy who rated his female classmates on a "Hot or Not" site created by one of his friends. He thought it was funny, but

Organizations like Cyber Mentors in the United Kingdom use Web site programming online to help teens deal with cyberbullies.

had no idea what he'd written would be sent around to the whole school for all the girls to read. He was dismayed to see some of the girls crying about it the next day, but he was most distressed to find out his younger sister had been added to the site after he'd seen it. "She was crying when I got home and wouldn't even look at me," he says.

"I think the kids can really empathize with the boy," Smith says.

The Mob Phenomenon

That's because most kids aren't intentionally vicious. Educators acknowledge that there will always be bullies who often have problems that require counseling and parental intervention, but many kids simply get roped in by the bullies.

"A lot of other kids get involved because it seems fun and they don't really understand the effect of what they're doing, until it snowballs," says Caitlin Johnson, editor of bNetS@vvy (www.bnetsavvy.org), a newsletter designed to help kids stay safer online, sponsored by the NEA [National Education Association] Health Information Network. "There's a 'pile on' mentality that can quickly escalate so that the victim feels the whole school is against them."

That's why experts agree that addressing the bystander is the best way to curb cyberbullying. By encouraging the bystander to have the courage to intervene rather than take part, most incidents of cyberbullying would fizzle before catching fire online.

"We must focus on peer leadership, or bystander, strategies," says Nancy Willard. "Peers have the ability to support the bully—directly or by their silence—or to challenge the bully by refusing to take part."

She also recommends emphasizing the behavior of the students, regardless of the technology they're using. "We may not understand or engage in cyberspace the way these children can, but they're not developmentally ready to consistently make good decisions about how they use it. As adults, our area of expertise is in human relations, behavior, and effective problem-solving. This is the insight our children and teens need from us."

TEN

Cyberbullies Should Be Held Accountable for Victims Who Commit Suicide

Robert Patrick and Joel Currier

> Robert Patrick and Joel Currier, reporters for *The St. Louis Post-Dispatch*, write here about federal charges that were filed against an adult, Lori Drew, who used MySpace to bully a teen girl, Megan Meier. Megan committed suicide soon after reading the last message that Drew sent to her. About six months after these charges were filed, Drew was found guilty of three misdemeanors in a jury trial.

For the parents of Megan Meier, the criminal charges handed down in California were a validation, finally, that their daughter's suicide deserved justice.

For Lori Drew, Megan's one-time neighbor and the target of the federal indictment, the charges were anything but justice—more like a flimsy legal move from clear across the country, her lawyer said.

And for U.S. Attorney Thomas O'Brien, the charges were a clear message about the tragic consequences of cyber bullying.

Those charges [in May 2008] moved the 2006 death of 13-year-old Megan, of Dardenne Prairie [Missouri] before the federal court system and back into the national spotlight.

The Federal Charges

O'Brien called a news conference in Los Angeles to announce the grand jury indictment against Drew: one count of conspiracy and three counts of illegally accessing MySpace computers "that she used to inflict emotional distress on a child." Prosecutors were

Lori Drew was indicted by a federal grand jury for the Internet harassment of thirteen-year-old Megan Meier that led to the girl's suicide.

able to file the charges in Los Angeles because the MySpace social networking site has its headquarters in the area. The key allegation: Drew helped create a fake MySpace profile and used it to harass Megan.

The indictment came more than 18 months after Megan received an e-mail telling her, "The world would be a better place without you," then hanged herself in her bedroom. She thought the message was from a boy with whom she had struck up an online relationship. The boy didn't exist.

Prosecutors are using a novel approach—applying a law used mainly to go after computer hackers—in a case that has come to symbolize Internet harassment.

But Megan's father, Ron Meier, was not worried about legal strategies. . . .

He sat at his kitchen table beside his girlfriend watching Megan's smiling image flash across a television screen. He couldn't wait to hear what the news anchor had to say.

"Part of me thought it would never happen," he said about the criminal charges against Drew.

The Protest

Dean Steward, one of Drew's attorneys, called the charges "creative," and vowed to try to get the case thrown out.

"How do you take these facts and jam it into the statute that they've apparently jammed it into?" he said.

He also said that he would challenge the venue.

"Why is this in Los Angeles?" he said. "How is it that the local prosecutor and the U.S. attorney (in St. Louis) looked at it and found no crime?"

Federal prosecutors in St. Louis and the St. Charles County prosecutor passed on trying to build a case.

O'Brien's office, though, took its own look at the case. . . .

O'Brien said Drew and unnamed "co-conspirators" violated MySpace's rules and terms of service by using false information to set up an account.

They used that account to obtain Megan's personal information and proceeded to "harass" Megan, O'Brien said, in an act with "horrendous ramifications."

Prosecutors are relying on a federal fraud statute that is typically used against people who steal information from government, law enforcement or military computers. They said this was the first time the statute is being used to prosecute a case of deception on a social networking site.

Sal Hernandez, assistant director of the FBI's [Federal Bureau of Investigation's] Los Angeles office, said Drew and the others "exploited a young girl's weakness."

"This case is just another lesson teaching us that malicious acts may have unforeseen consequences," Hernandez said.

Drew was asked to turn herself in . . . in St. Louis. If convicted, she could face five years in prison for each charge, although her lawyer said that more than a year total would be unlikely.

The Messages' Tragic Results

The indictment says Drew and her co-conspirators in September 2006 set up a bogus MySpace account—that of a 16-year-old boy named Josh Evans—and used a fake photo.

The co-conspirators of Drew, who used to run a coupon book business, are not named. But Drew's former employee, Ashley Grills, told *Good Morning America* . . . that she, Drew and Drew's daughter created the account to find out what Megan was saying (Grills told the program that she'd been granted immunity in exchange for her cooperation in the case).

Megan and the Drews' daughter had been friends but had a falling-out. The Drews heard that Megan was talking about their daughter.

"Josh Evans" struck up an online relationship with Megan, whose parents have said had long struggled with depression. Josh and Megan chatted for a few weeks.

On October 7, Megan got a message informing her that Josh was moving away.

Megan wrote back to Josh and later gave him a cell phone number and wrote, "I love you so much," the indictment says.

Examples of Cyberbullying

1. **Flaming:** Online fights using electronic messages with angry and vulgar language

2. **Harassment:** Repeatedly sending nasty, mean, and insulting messages

3. **Denigration:** Sending or posting gossip or rumors about a person to damage his or her reputation or friendships

4. **Impersonation:** Pretending to be someone else and sending or posting material to get that person in trouble or in danger; or to damage that person's reputation or friendships

5. **Outing:** Sharing someone's secrets or embarrassing information or images online

6. **Trickery:** Talking someone into revealing secrets or embarrassing information, then sharing it online

7. **Exclusion:** Intentionally and cruelly excluding someone from an online group

8. **Cyberstalking:** Repeated, intense harassment and denigration that includes threats or causes significant fear

Taken from: Nancy Willard, "Educator's Guide to Cyberbullying and Cyberthreats." www.cyberbully.org/cyberbully/docs/cbcteducator.pdf.

Then, on Oct. 16, Megan got a final message. Grills, who was 18 at the time, told ABC that she typed it: "The world would be a better place without you."

"Within an hour of receiving that last message . . . Megan Meier went up to her bedroom and hanged herself," O'Brien said at the news conference.

Lori Drew and the co-conspirators later deleted the Josh Evans account, the indictment says, and Drew told a child who knew about the account "to keep her mouth shut."

Steward, Drew's lawyer, said his client never typed any of the messages, although she was aware of the MySpace page.

He also said that there are "a number" of bogus claims about the case that have been floated on the Internet.

Last year [2007], St. Charles County Prosecuting Attorney Jack Banas said the circumstances surrounding Megan's death did not amount to a state crime. [In April 2008], he said his opinion has not changed.

U.S. Attorney Catherine Hanaway said . . . the only possible charge her office thought would apply was "transmitting a threat." But she said her office had worked with O'Brien's and said that she was "pleased that there's a prosecution that's being brought."

Are the Charges Acceptable?

Heidi Rummel, a former federal prosecutor in Los Angeles who is now a law professor at the University of Southern California [USC] questioned the charges against Drew.

"What they did seems horrible in retrospect, given that it resulted in a suicide, but are the federal criminal statutes the way to address that harm?" she asked.

"It's taking teenage gossip and banter to another level, but we've never criminalized that conduct," Rummel added.

Another USC law professor, Rebecca Lonergan, also questioned the use of the fraud statute.

"I'm not sure that the plain language of this statute covers the conduct that took place here," she said.

Ron Meier said he hopes the charges force the Drews to feel some of "the pain and suffering that I'm going to feel for the rest of my life."

He and his wife, Tina, started divorce proceedings months after Megan's death. That divorce is almost final.

Tina Meier said . . . she was thrilled about the indictment: "I've been waiting a year and a half for some vindication."

Tina, once a real estate agent, is now working full time as head of the Megan Meier Foundation, touring the country to speak about suicide and Internet harassment.

"Bottom line," she said, "is that there is finally a court system that believes in this case."

ELEVEN

Open Communication in the Classroom Can Help Prevent Teen Suicides

Douglas Fisher

Douglas Fisher is a professor of language and literacy education at San Diego State University. He wrote this article for *The Phi Delta Kappan*, a professional journal for educators at all levels. Fisher encourages educators to be aware of the warning signs of teen suicide and to deliberately encourage students to talk about this difficult topic by suggesting or requiring students to read books that address the issue. He also discusses what to do if a student's writing presents itself as a warning sign for suicide.

What comes to mind when you think of the word adolescence? First dates? A driver's license? Hormones? If you are the teacher of one of the more than 500,000 young people who attempt suicide or the 5,000 who succeed in committing suicide each year, your view of adolescence may be a bit less jovial. Every two hours and 15 minutes, a person under the age of 25 completes a suicide. Since suicide is one of the leading causes of death for young people between the ages of 15 and 19, it's hard to imagine a high school teacher who hasn't been touched by this epidemic.

The issue is of such national significance that in September 2004, more than 350 members of the U.S. House of Representatives and the entire U.S. Senate voted to pass the Garrett Lee Smith

Douglas Fisher, "Keeping Adolescents 'Alive and Kickin' It': Addressing Suicide in Schools," *Phi Delta Kappan*, vol. 87, June 2006, pp. 784–86. Reproduced by permission of the publisher and the author.

Memorial Act, bipartisan legislation to reduce youth suicide. The bill authorized $82 million over three years for screening, assessment, and counseling.

While this seems like a great deal of money and it will certainly help educators address the problem of adolescent suicide, it will not work unless classroom teachers and building administrators serve as an early warning system. As teachers and administrators, we must be on the watch for the signs of adolescent suicide, and we must know how to respond when we come face to face with this daunting reality. Furthermore, we must confront this epidemic and provide space within schools for students to disclose their feelings to a trusting adult. Together with social services and healthcare providers, we can help reduce the toll of youth suicide.

The Warning Signs

According to the American Association of Suicidology (www .suicidology.org), approximately 80% of the people who attempt or succeed in committing suicide showed advance warning signs. Some of the signs of potential suicide in teens include:

- talking about committing suicide,
- having trouble eating or sleeping,
- experiencing drastic changes in behavior,
- withdrawing from friends and/ or social activities,
- giving away prized possessions,
- having attempted suicide before,
- taking unnecessary risks,
- being preoccupied with death and dying,
- losing interest in personal appearance, and
- increasing use of alcohol or drugs.

Being gay, lesbian, bisexual, or transgendered or adjusting to feelings of attraction to members of the same sex may also present an increased suicide risk.

There are a number of issues for teachers and administrators to consider when such signs are present. Students disclose information about themselves in a number of ways, including in their conversations with peers and adults, in their writing, and in their behavior. How should we respond when we observe these early warning signs? Again, it is important to remember that teachers and administrators can serve as the early warning system that alerts the social and health services system to a youth in need. Most adolescent students do not know their school nurse, social worker, or psychologist very well. They often trust a teacher and reveal their problems to him or her first. As a result, despite a lack of training or support, the teacher becomes the broker of services for youths at risk of suicide.

Creating School Talk

By the time they have reached adolescence, students know which topics are "off-limits" in school. While some students will discuss and write about things that matter in their lives, they are more likely to do so when such topics are seen as permissible. There are a number of ways educators can subtly inform students that they can discuss the issues that consume their thinking.

One common way to ensure that students know that they can discuss delicate issues with their teachers is to provide them access to books and information that explore these topics. These books can be in the school library or in a classroom library. In some cases, a teacher may give a specific book to a student to communicate that "you can talk with me about this." . . . It is important to note that, like much of the recently published adolescent fiction, these books [that deal with suicide] pull no punches and directly address the issues that our adolescents are struggling with.

As a case in point, Jerome (all names here are pseudonyms) was reading *The Burn Journals* and said, "Man, I thought I had it bad. This guy hates life. I want to be alive and kickin' it." Colin was reading *Jay's Journal* when he said to his teacher, "Everyone at this school has thought out about it [suicide]. I get picked on 'cuz I'm so small and all. . . . I've thought about it. But Jay didn't know that death is a permanent solution to a temporary problem."

The teachers and administrators at Hoover High School in San Diego decided to address the issue more directly. During the opening weeks of school, the sustained silent reading period,

Adolescent Literature That Addresses Suicide

• Terri Fields, *After the Death of Anna Gonzales*. New York: Henry Holt, 2002.	• Walter Dean Myers, *Shooter*. New York: HarperTempest, 2004.
• Paul Fleischman, *Whirligig*. New York: Henry Holt, 1998.	• Brent Runyon, *The Burn Journals*. New York: Alfred A. Knopf, 2004.
• E.R. Frank, *Life Is Funny*. New York: Dorling Kindersley, 2000.	• Beatrice Sparks, ed., *Jay's Journal*. New York: Pocket Books, 1979.
• E.R. Frank, *America*. New York: Simon Pulse, 2002.	• Terry Trueman, *Inside Out*. New York: HarperTempest, 2003.
• John Green, *Looking for Alaska*. New York: Penguin, 2005.	• Ellen Wittlinger, *Razzle*. New York: Simon Pulse, 2001.
• Shelly Fraser Mickle, *The Turning Hour*. Montgomery, AL: River City, 2001.	

Taken from: Douglas Fisher, "Keeping Adolescents 'Alive and Kickin' It': Addressing Suicide in Schools." *Phi Delta Kappan*, vol. 87, no. 10, June 2006.

which occurs for 20 minutes each day, was suspended. During this time, every teacher read aloud the book *Whirligig*. A total of 2,300 students heard this book and discussed it with their teachers. In the first chapter, Brent goes to a party, is rejected, drunk, and attempts suicide by closing his eyes and taking his hands off the steering wheel. Of course, discussing this book schoolwide meant that the school had to be ready for students to discuss drinking, drinking and driving, and suicide. In many places, these would be forbidden topics. However, the Hoover faculty wanted students to know that these were real issues and that every student had a support system available.

Several days into the reading of *Whirligig*, Anna showed up in the classroom of one of her teachers with the book in her hand.

She pointed to the line in which Brent attempts suicide and said, "This is me. I've tried this. I've tried it a lot." Fortunately, her teacher knew how to respond to the situation and convinced Anna to enroll herself in a support group for battered girls and a counseling program offered at the school.

When a Life Depends on It

Certainly students' anxieties, concerns, and worries enter into the classroom discourse in a variety of ways and on a regular basis. As teachers, we can try to avoid these situations of disclosure by avoiding any personal conversations with students, either in writing or in discussions. Yet despite our efforts to steer clear of risky topics, they are inevitable and unavoidable. As Marti Singer noted, "Once we have read a paper, there is a contract between us and the person. . . . We need to respect the students' possible anxiety in telling the story at all . . . we need to ascertain what the writer needs and what our role is to be—advice-giver, classifier, info-giver, listener, facilitator, friend."

In 1995, Marilyn Valentino described the ways that teachers commonly respond to students' writing. While her focus was on writing, these behavioral patterns can be seen in any student/teacher discussions. Consider the following five approaches:

- The Ostrich Approach: ignore the comment altogether and say to yourself, "There is no problem. There is no problem."
- The Rush Limbaugh Approach: note the errors but ignore the content, as in "You missed an *i* in suicide."
- The Sally Jessy Rafael Approach: encourage more information and further disclosure without addressing the issue and providing guidance.
- The Dr. Quinn Approach: overreact, use "antiquated medicine to heal the patient," and misinterpret a need.
- The Professional Approach: recognize the pain while offering help and professional assistance and asking the person what he or she would like you to do.

Students who exhibit the warning signs of suicide need to have teachers adopt a professional approach. Thankfully, Anna's teacher knew this. As teachers and administrators, we have to become comfortable responding in this way to our students. In addition, students who have lost someone to suicide can benefit from writing about their thoughts, emotions, reactions, and experiences. In other words, writing can both allow us to identify students at risk and be therapeutic for students.

When Not to Keep a Secret

Formal writing interventions can also be used to identify students at risk for suicide. One such initiative, an essay project of the American Psychiatric Association Alliance, is titled "When Not to Keep a Secret" and was developed in response to fears of school violence. The idea was to provide students with a formal opportunity to consider when keeping a secret was harmful. The instruction and associated writing enable students to reflect on their experiences in breaking a confidence and trusting an adult. While the program was developed to address school violence, approximately 90% of the papers submitted focus on suicide. (More information on this initiative can be found at www.apa alliance.org; click on "Projects.")

The American Psychiatric Association Alliance has partnered with the Yellow Ribbon Campaign in its efforts to prevent suicide. The Yellow Ribbon Campaign provides guest speakers, training, online advice, an 800 hotline, request-for-help cards, and information across the country (www.yellow ribbon.org). Inviting guest speakers into schools is another way to help students understand that they are not alone in their experiences, thoughts, and needs and that there are adults around them who care.

While there are much happier topics I could have written about—from using graphic novels to engage struggling readers, to problem-based learning as a motivational tool, to establishing high expectations for all students—I believe that we educators must confront the issue of adolescent suicide directly.

Students at Shiprock High School in New Hampshire participate in a suicide prevention workshop that challenges them to work on personal development and to spot the warning signs of suicide.

We must not follow the path of least resistance, the "ostrich approach." Nor should we blame the victim and his or her parents. Instead, we must provide students with an opportunity to seek and receive the help they need as they negotiate the trials, tribulations, and triumphs of adolescence.

TWELVE

Crisis Hotlines Can Help Prevent Suicides

John Draper

> John Draper is the project director for the National Suicide Prevention Lifeline. *Behavioral Healthcare* is the practical resource on technology, reimbursement, and treatment trends for managers and clinicians in the mental health and substance abuse fields. In this article, Draper writes about the importance of suicide crisis hotlines, stressing that they can supplement emergency room visits, fill the gap when behavioral health care systems in communities are overburdened, and reach people who are in remote areas or are unable to leave their homes.

When it comes to preventing suicide, every minute counts. Every minute in the United States, a person makes a suicide attempt. Every 16 minutes, a person ends his/her life. Each minute, then, becomes an opportunity to provide immediate mental healthcare and prevent a person from dying by suicide.

A growing network of community health centers, community mental health centers, nonprofit organizations, and other facilities provide care when people are facing suicidal crises. Lives are saved because of the dedicated professionals who staff these care centers, from doctors and nurses to counselors and therapists. Yet, few centers have the resources to operate 24 hours a day, 7 days a week. Mental health counselors and other care providers face the difficult task of providing their patients with adequate resources for after-hours help, sometimes in communities where the hospital emergency department (ED) is the only option if a crisis occurs during nontraditional hours. Care providers also need resources to give to people in crisis and their family members to explain what to do when they cannot access traditional methods of care. For example, what should people do when they lack transportation to get to their appointments or during a crisis when they need immediate support?

Research shows that EDs treat the majority of suicide attempt survivors. Every year, many thousands of people facing a suicidal crisis seek care in EDs because they offer around-the-clock care and open access. While EDs can provide some immediate help, they often are overused and inappropriate as a "first option" for people in emotional crisis and considering suicide.

Emergency Department Shortcomings

EDs typically are designed to provide assessment for hospital admission and while psychotropic medications frequently are dispensed for ED discharges, EDs are not best suited for therapeutic interventions and supportive counseling assistance. It can be extremely difficult for overburdened EDs to provide the full range of services that people in crisis need; 90% of those who die by suicide have a treatable mental illness but require care beyond what they received in the ED.

Suicide attempters who have been admitted to hospitals can fall between the cracks postdischarge, never reaching the community-based mental health services that the hospital has referred them to in their discharge plan. Recent research has shown that the risk of suicide only one week after discharge from psychiatric hospitalization is up to 102 times higher for males and 60 times higher for females when compared to the general population's risk, indicating a need for rapid, efficient aftercare

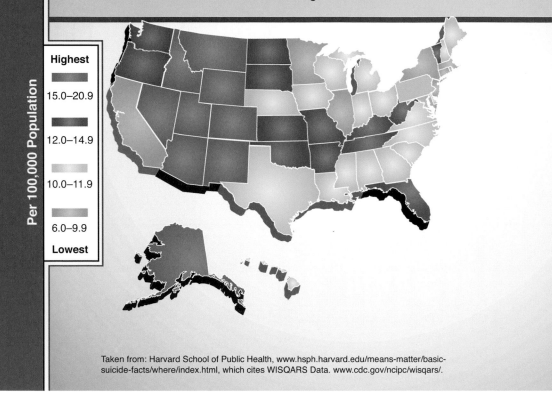

Suicide by State, 2000–2004

Suicide rates are highest in rural areas, in the West, (excluding California) and, to a lesser extent, in parts of the South and northern New England.

Per 100,000 Population

Highest

15.0–20.9

12.0–14.9

10.0–11.9

6.0–9.9

Lowest

Taken from: Harvard School of Public Health, www.hsph.harvard.edu/means-matter/basic-suicide-facts/where/index.html, which cites WISQARS Data. www.cdc.gov/ncipc/wisqars/.

linkages to community mental health services. Unfortunately, if recent findings from California are any indication, ED personnel report a remarkable lack of community mental health resources with which to refer high-risk patients. So how can ED staff, inpatient discharge planners, and community mental health service providers fill these potentially fatal gaps in our behavioral health systems?

While crisis hotline services are not the only answer, they are a critical, underutilized resource for filling service gaps and supporting people at risk in overburdened community behavioral health systems. Crisis lines, such as many of the certified call centers participating in the federally funded National Suicide Prevention Lifeline network, offer 24/7 access to trained workers who can provide assessment, supportive counseling, and crisis intervention for people in emotional or suicidal distress in communities across America.

Research indicates the potential value of crisis lines in filling treatment access and continuing care gaps in behavioral health systems. New findings have shown that crisis call centers can reduce emotional distress and suicidality in callers, with clear indications that lives have been saved. Other research has shown that utilizing call center services to provide follow-up care post-discharge from EDs has positive effects on people with mental health problems, including enhancing treatment linkages and reducing emotional distress and suicide attempts. Furthermore, clients receiving community mental healthcare can benefit from using hotlines between therapy sessions. [One study] demonstrated that at times patients were more open to telephone contact than an in-person appointment at a psychiatric clinic.

Reaching the Unreachable

Because of their unique all-hours, in-home accessibility to trained counselors, crisis hotlines provide a means of delivering behavioral health services to clients who may be unwilling or unable to seek or maintain care in traditional behavioral health settings. Uninsured people and individuals living in remote areas, along with crises occurring at any time, necessitate ready access to affordable mental health supports at all hours. In some cases, expecting people who have major depression, agoraphobia, or other disabling mental health conditions to leave their homes (or beds) to attend outpatient sessions could be analogous to putting a spinal cord injury clinic at the top of a steep staircase, as a colleague in the telephone counseling business put it. Clearly, crisis lines can be a critical supplement to expanding community behavioral health delivery options for the wide range of illnesses and functional impairments that confront our systems of care.

The Lifeline, 1-800-273-TALK, is a network of 120 local certified crisis call centers across the country that can provide 24/7 assistance to people facing suicidal crises. The Lifeline is a resource for traditional community behavioral health agencies that want to ensure that suicidal individuals have access to mental health resources before, during, and after a crisis. Callers typically receive supportive counseling, assessment, resource information, and referrals—including emergency service linkages—from trained helpers at the network center closest to their area.

The Lifeline utilizes research and consultation from national experts in suicide prevention to promote the use of best practices among its network of centers. The Lifeline recently developed national research-based standards for suicide risk assessments to

In the United States a person commits suicide every sixteen minutes. Suicide prevention hotlines provide services in which people can discuss their problems with a trained counselor.

guide the work of its member centers, to better ensure that callers at high risk are identified and receive appropriate assistance. The Lifeline network also is providing evidence-informed trainings to support the implementation of best practices among its network centers.

The Lifeline also offers support to providers—the dedicated doctors, counselors, nurses—the EMTs [emergency medical technicians] and behavioral health specialists who work every day to promote mental health and prevent suicide. The Lifeline and many of its local crisis centers stand ready to partner with these and other groups. It is essential that strong links are established between traditional care providers and local crisis call centers and/or the Lifeline so that 24/7 intervention and support services may be accessible to those in suicidal crisis.

Working Together to Save Lives

With these partnerships in place, hospitals and other traditional care centers can better use crisis hotlines to provide continuity of care for attempt survivors and/or other high-risk individuals they serve (or are discharging). The partnership opportunities between hospital or community-based services and crisis call centers are substantial, ranging from utilizing local call centers to provide follow-up care postdischarge or between therapy sessions, to contracting for after-clinic-hours assistance (a frequent use of crisis lines). The Lifeline also provides free materials for people at risk for suicide, their families, the general public, and professional healthcare providers, which can be easily disseminated to clients or patients, or in community outreach efforts. . . .

Each year approximately 30,000 people die by suicide in the United States. Countless more individuals attempt suicide. Through the Lifeline network, we are building partnerships that have the power to provide a continuum of care to people facing suicidal crisis. By building these relationships, we are making the most of each minute and capturing every opportunity to prevent another friend or family member from needlessly being lost to suicide. Working together, we can prevent more suicide attempts and reduce the overall number of people lost to suicide every year.

THIRTEEN

High School Programs Can Prevent Teen Suicide

Stacy Teicher Khadaroo

Stacy Teicher Khadaroo is a staff writer for *The Christian Science Monitor*, an international daily newspaper. In this viewpoint she examines a suicide-prevention program for high schools. The program, Signs of Suicide (SOS), encourages students to talk about suicide, to recognize friends who may need help, and to act on that information. Schools that have used this program reportedly have significantly fewer suicide attempts among their students.

It may still be a taboo subject in society, but for freshmen at Medway High school, there's no avoiding frank talk about suicide.

In early December [2008], each of the roughly 240 students spent one of their double-period classes watching a video about depression and suicide presented by a counselor. After completing a self-screening survey, they could check off a box if they wanted to talk with someone about themselves or a friend. They left class with handouts reminding them to "ACT": "Acknowledge" if a friend has a problem; "Care" by letting him or her know you want to help; and "Tell" a trusted adult.

That's the key message of the Signs of Suicide (SOS) prevention program. Since 2000–01, more than 3,500 schools throughout the United States have used its materials and training kits to teach students how to recognize and respond to depression and suicidal thoughts.

"People are always telling me that the program has saved lives in their schools," says Sharon Pigeon, manager of SOS at Screening for Mental Health Inc., a nonprofit in Wellesley, Massachusetts.

Ms. Pigeon's own niece, 14 years old at the time, confided in her that a friend had attempted suicide and planned to "do it right" the next weekend. Using materials from SOS, Pigeon persuaded her niece that they should call the school counselor. "Later, the girl said to [my niece and other friends], 'I don't know which one of you told on me, but I'm glad you did because you saved my life,'" Pigeon says.

A Statistically Successful Program

Her anecdotes are backed up by independent research. SOS is the only school-based curriculum shown to reduce self-reported suicide attempts in randomized controlled studies.

While suicide by young people is rare, it's the third leading cause of death among 15- to 24-year-olds, according to the National Center for Injury Prevention and Control. Knowing the ripple effects that even one teen suicide can have in a community, educators are eager to equip students with tools like SOS.

Research reports in 2004 and 2007 found that suicide attempts were 40 percent less for students in the SOS high school program than for the control group. The results were similar across racial and socioeconomic groups. Because of such studies, SOS is listed on the National Registry of Effective Programs maintained by the US government's Substance Abuse and Mental Health Services Administration. Middle schools have started using an age-appropriate version of SOS recently as well.

The Massachusetts Department of Mental Health increased its funding for youth suicide prevention to $75,000 in 2007, up from $20,000 the year before. Most of the money is used to purchase SOS kits for hundreds of schools, and to train school staff. Educators are urged to build ties with community mental health

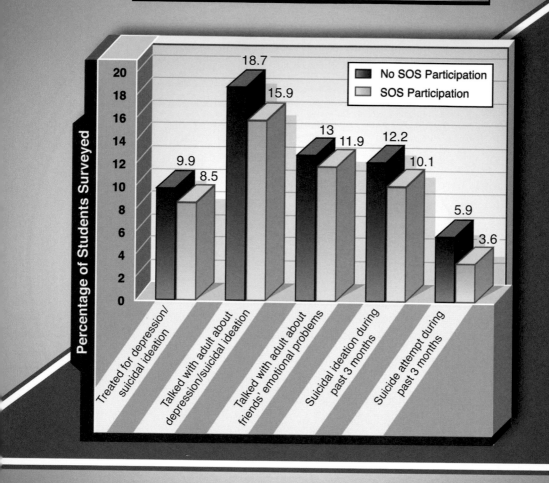

Outcomes of the Signs of Suicide (SOS) Prevention Program

Percentage of Students Surveyed

- No SOS Participation
- SOS Participation

	No SOS	SOS
Treated for depression/suicidal ideation	9.9	8.5
Talked with adult about depression/suicidal ideation	18.7	15.9
Talked with adult about friends' emotional problems	13	11.9
Suicidal ideation during past 3 months	12.2	10.1
Suicide attempt during past 3 months	5.9	3.6

Taken from: Robert H. Aseltine Jr. and Robert DeMartino, "An Outcome Evaluation of the SOS Suicide Prevention Program," *American Journal of Public Health*, March 2004, vol. 94, no. 3.

providers to make sure help is at hand once students start identifying peers as depressed or potentially suicidal.

Teachers frequently use the ACT acronym (Acknowledge, Care, Tell) to encourage students "not only to identify young people who may be suicidal, but also for such things as bullying and dating violence," says Alan Holmlund, director of the state's suicide prevention program.

A Student's Perspective

Sadie, a Medway senior who heard the SOS presentation as a sophomore, says that "in high school, especially in a small town like this, . . . once you break someone's trust you don't know where you're going to end up yourself." But SOS gives students a different perspective, she says. "You really see how dangerous it is not to speak out. . . . When it comes down to either losing a friend because they're not talking to you anymore or losing a friend because they lost their life, you know, I think this makes people come out and say, 'This person needs help.'"

Medway counselor Meredith Poulten sends a letter to parents each year explaining the SOS program and the basic self-screening survey that students are asked to take. After seeing the presentation, students privately answer a few questions about their mental outlook, ranging from "Do you have less energy than you normally do?" to "Do you think seriously about killing yourself?" Then a scoring guide tells them whether they should consider evaluation or counseling.

Each year Mrs. Poulten gets some calls from parents with questions, and a few decide they don't want their children to participate. Usually less than 1 percent of students say they want to talk with a counselor after the screening. But Poulten finds about a dozen whose surveys prompt her to "check to make sure they're OK," she says. "Sometimes they're just having a bad day. If we do really find a problem, then we contact the parents."

Poulten runs a drop-in center where students can come to talk, hang out, or even do research for a class. While she encourages them to talk over issues with parents, she keeps everything confidential unless students are at risk of harming themselves or others. She also oversees peer counselors, who assist with the SOS program and have their own room where students can come talk about anything on their minds.

A Student's Plea

Perhaps the most effective component of SOS at Medway is an additional video created by a peer counselor who has since graduated.

Looking straight into the camera, occasionally flipping wavy blond hair out of his eyes, he tells what led to his own suicide attempts in high school.

Depression and suicidal thoughts are "kind of like a black hole. . . . It gradually gets bigger and bigger and sucks you in until everything is just a negative thought," he says to the somber freshmen watching him on a screen. He describes the night when he got into a fight not only with his best friend but with his parents, too. He stormed into his room after telling his family, "I'm sorry for making your life so difficult . . . and hopefully you can find someone to take my place and be a lot better than I've been."

Nobody checked on him, as he hoped they would. "That night I cut myself worse than I'd ever cut myself before, hoping that I wouldn't wake up in the morning. I thank God every day that I

The suicide prevention program Signs of Suicide encourages students to talk to counselors to get help with their problems.

woke up, now," he says. He tried to hang himself that summer, but the following school year Poulten's message started to click and he realized "that people needed me around, and I had things to do and accomplish."

His plea to each freshman at Medway (where a girl succeeded in her suicide attempt while he was a student there): "Look at your friends, notice what's going on. . . . This isn't a joke."

The Truth Sinking In

After the videos, the class is quiet. Poulten invites questions and discussion, but she doesn't push when there's no verbal response. Many students nod when asked if they would feel comfortable talking to an adult about a friend exhibiting the signs they've just learned about. A few say the Medway student's video was easier to relate to than the SOS video, in which actors play out scenes and the right and wrong way to react to a friend exhibiting various warning signs.

Their English teacher, Laura Morris, wonders if the message really sank in for these honors students. "I saw them kind of smirking and laughing. . . . I was wondering, how can kids get over that sense of 'Oh, that's silly, that's for the kids who are messed up'?"

Most students do take the message seriously, Poulten and the peer counselors say. It's difficult to know if the absence of suicide at Medway in the past few years has been because of SOS. But Poulten has seen an increase in students referring their friends to her.

"We hope that this has a long-lasting effect. At least it's in the back of their mind . . . that there's help and if the subject [of suicide] comes up, and what they can do about it," she says.

What You Should Know About Teen Suicide

The Prevalence of Teen Suicides

Suicides occur at an alarming rate among young people and at a much higher rate than the general population. The American Association of Suicidology reports that:

- Suicide is the third leading cause of death among 15- to 24-year-olds. Only accidents and homicides take more lives than suicides among people in this age group.
- In 2005, 32,637 people completed suicide; 4,212 of these people were 15- to 24-year-olds.
- Each year in the United States, 1.3 percent of all deaths result from suicides. The suicide rate among 15- to 24-year-olds is much higher at 12.3 percent of all deaths.
- Every 2 hours and 11 minutes, someone under the age of 25 commits suicide in the United States.
- Every day, approximately 12 young people commit suicide.
- Every year, 10 out of every 100,000 young people commit suicide.

Trends in Suicide Rates

According to the American Association of Suicidology:

- Since 1950, the suicide rate for 15- to 24-year-old males has quadrupled and for females has doubled.
- From 1980 to 1994, the suicide rate for 15- to 24-year-olds increased by 19 percent.

- The suicide rate peaked in 1994 with 11 suicides per 100,000 young people.
- Since 1994, suicides have decreased by 34 percent, with the rate at 8.2 per 100,000 in 2004.

The Prevalence of Suicide Among Minority Teens

According to the Tennessee Commission on Children and Youth:
- The suicide rate among black teens aged 15 to 19 more than doubled between 1980 and 1995. More recent statistics report that about five black teens die from suicides every day.
- One-fourth of all teen suicide victims in the United States are Hispanic American.
- Some studies have reported significantly higher rates of suicide attempts among gay and lesbian youth—20 to 39 percent, compared to 5 to 10 percent of teens in the general population.

Gender Disparities in Teen Suicide

Teen girls attempt suicide three times more than teen boys, but teen boys die from suicide four times more often. This is probably because girls tend to use a method from which there is a greater possibility of rescue, such as overdosing on drugs or cutting themselves, whereas boys more often choose a method involving firearms, hanging, or jumping from great heights, according to Body and Health Canada.

The Prevalence of Suicidal Thoughts and Plans

- According to a Gallup poll, 45 percent of all teens aged 13 to 17 reported personally knowing a peer who has attempted suicide.

The Youth Risk Behavior Survey released in 2008 by the U.S. Centers for Disease Control and Prevention reports that in the twelve months before their survey conducted in 2007:
- Nationwide, 28.5 percent of all students felt so sad and hopeless that they ceased participating in some usual activity almost every day for at least two weeks.

- Nationwide, 14.5 percent of all students considered attempting suicide. Suicidal thoughts were significantly more prevalent among females (18.7 percent) than males (10.3 percent). Tenth-grade females (22 percent) and Hispanic females (21.1 percent) reported the highest rates.
- Nationwide, 11.3 percent of all students made a suicide plan. Suicide plans were most prevalent among tenth-grade females (16.1 percent) and Hispanic females (15.2 percent).
- Nearly 7 percent of all students had attempted suicide at least once, with the highest rate among Hispanic females at 14 percent.
- Nationwide, 2 percent of all students attempted a suicide resulting in a visit to a doctor or nurse, with the highest rate among Hispanic females at nearly 4 percent.

Risk Factors for Teen Suicide

Certain stressful conditions, events and situations can increase the likelihood of a suicidal act, especially if these conditions combine. According to the office of the U.S. Surgeon General some of these are:
- Alcohol or substance abuse
- Mental health problems, especially bipolar disorder or mood disorder
- Former suicide attempts
- The tendency to be aggressive or impulsive
- Access to firearms
- Significant disappointment, loss of status, or humiliation, such as a breakup, an unplanned pregnancy, or incarceration
- The death or suicide of a loved one

Warning Signs for Teen Suicide

Eight in ten people who commit suicide give clues that they want to kill themselves.

According to the American Psychological Association, warning signs of potential self-violence include:
- Changes in mood or behavior, such as increased moodiness or withdrawal

- Major changes in sleeping or eating habits
- Drop in grades or decreased interest in school
- Lack of interest in usual activities
- Increased conflict with authority figures
- Perfectionism
- Feelings of hopelessness, guilt, or worthlessness
- Giving away belongings
- Talking about death, dying, the afterlife, or talking about suicidal plans
- Saying good-bye or hinting at not being here in the future

Factors That Protect Teens from Suicide

According to the Connecticut Youth Suicide Advisory Board, the following can reduce the likeliness of suicide:

- Easy access to mental health services
- Family and community support
- Problem-solving and conflict-resolution skills
- Religious and cultural beliefs that support self-preservation and discourage suicide

What You Should Do About Teen Suicide

With a reported 17 percent of teens having thought about, 13 percent having planned, and 8 percent having attempted suicide, it is probably more likely than not that you know well or are at least acquainted with someone who seriously thinks about suicide. Unfortunately, we often don't realize that someone is thinking about suicide until it is too late.

If one of your friends threatened to commit suicide, what would you do?

- Would you ignore it?
- Would you assume that your friend just wanted attention?
- Would you think that if the friend was serious about it, he or she wouldn't be talking about it?
- Would you tell your friend not to say things like that?

If you reacted in one of these ways, you might be missing a chance to save a friend's life.

Suicide is difficult to understand and not something that is easy to talk about. However, because teens are more likely to confide in and to listen to other teens, suicide is a topic worth understanding and talking about.

Understand Suicide

While it is difficult to predict who will commit suicide, most people who commit suicide or who have suicidal ideation (think about killing themselves) are suffering from depression, a very real mental health disorder. The good news is that depression—even depression that results in suicidal ideation—is a very treatable disorder. Should someone close to you speak of wanting to harm themselves or state that the world would be better off without them, your sympathetic listening in a nonjudgmental way as well as your emotional support is valuable and important. However, it is also important for the depressed person to obtain the help of a mental health professional—a psychologist, a psychiatrist, or a professional social worker is invaluable and can assist in bringing some much-needed help.

Know the Signs and Risk Factors of Suicide

Besides direct and indirect threats, there are many other warning signs to look for. And while the warning signs may be different for different people, there are some overall trends to look for. There may be changes in personality or behavior that seem inconsistent with a person's general demeanor, such as a normally outgoing person suddenly becoming withdrawn; or perhaps the opposite—a quiet or reserved person suddenly engaging in "wild" or dangerous behavior. The breaking off of significant relationships (breaking up with a boy/girlfriend, end of a friendship, etc.) or other significant losses (like the death of a loved one, or even the news of not being accepted at the college of her/his "dreams," etc.) may precipitate suicidal ideation or severe depression.

Listen and Respond

An estimated eight out of ten people who commit suicide give some kind of warning beforehand, and it is a myth that people talk about suicide mostly to get attention. Should someone you know state either explicitly or vaguely that they are considering harming themselves, listen to them. Even indirect threats like "nothing matters" and "I won't see you again" should be taken seriously. Let them know you hear them. Let them know that you care and that there is no reason to feel embarrassed or ashamed by their feelings. No threat of suicide should ever be taken lightly.

Tell Someone and Ask for Help

Recommend that they speak with parents or other adults who can be trusted—school counselors are trained to deal with such situations. Certainly, a mental health professional should be consulted, as depression can be successfully treated.

If the person is in immediate danger—they have the means of hurting themselves at hand and are threatening to do so—immediately call for help. Dial 911. The police and emergency medical personnel are trained in handling such situations. Perhaps the individual will willingly go with you to an emergency room—that is another place to go where there are trained individuals prepared to handle such situations.

Be an Advocate for Suicide Prevention

Speak with school counselors and other members of the administration about establishing resources for students who may be troubled by depression. These important adults in the educational system are familiar with community resources and other venues of help for young people. They are also in a unique position to help educate other young people about the warning signs of depression and suicide ideation and to offer direction in helping those most at risk.

The editors have compiled the following list of organizations concerned with the issues debated in this book. The descriptions are derived from materials provided by the organizations. All have publications or information available for interested readers. The list was compiled on the date of publication of the present volume; the information provided here may change. Be aware that many organizations take several weeks or longer to respond to inquiries, so allow as much time as possible.

American Academy of Child and Adolescent Psychiatry (AACAP)

3615 Wisconsin Ave. NW, Washington, DC 20016-3007
(202) 966-7300 • fax: (202) 966-2891
e-mail: communications@aacap.org
Web site: www.aacap.org

The AACAP is a member-based professional organization composed of over seventy-five hundred child and adolescent psychiatrists and other interested physicians. It widely distributes information in an effort to promote understanding of mental illnesses and remove the stigma associated with them, advance efforts in prevention of mental illnesses, and assure proper treatment and access to services for children and adolescents. It publishes the parenting guides *Your Child* and *Your Adolescent*. Other publications for families include fact sheets, informational videos, and a glossary of symptoms and mental illnesses, which are all available through its Web site.

American Association of Suicidology (AAS)

5221 Wisconsin Ave. NW, Washington, DC 20015
(202) 237-2280 • fax: (202) 237-2282
e-mail: www.suicidology.org/web/guest/contact-us
Web site: www.suicidology.org

The association is one of the largest suicide-prevention organizations in the United States. AAS promotes the view that suicidal thoughts are almost always a symptom of depression and that suicide is almost never a rational decision. In addition to focusing on the prevention of suicide, the group also works to increase public awareness about suicide and to help those grieving the death of a loved one to suicide. The association publishes the quarterly newsletters *American Association of Suicidology—Newslink* and *Surviving Suicide*, and the quarterly journal *Suicide and Life Threatening Behavior*.

American Psychiatric Association (APA)

1000 Wilson Blvd., Ste. 1825, Arlington, VA 22209-3901
(703) 907-7300
e-mail: apa@psych.org
Web site: www.psych.org

An organization of psychiatrists dedicated to studying the nature, treatment, and prevention of mental disorders, the APA helps create mental health policies, distributes information about psychiatry, and promotes psychiatric research and education. It publishes the *American Journal of Psychiatry* and *Psychiatric News* monthly.

American Psychological Association (APA)

750 First St. NE, Washington, DC 20002-4242
(202) 336-5500
e-mail: public.affairs@apa.org
Web site: www.apa.org • www.apahelpcenter.org/

This professional organization for psychologists aims to advance psychology as a science, as a profession, and as a means of promoting human welfare. It produces the journal *American Psychologist* as well as numerous publications available online, including the monthly newsletter *Monitor on Psychology* and press releases, such as "Suicidal Thoughts Among College Students More Common than Expected." The APA also provides articles, fact sheets, and interactive features such as "Mind/Body Health" for the general public at its Web site.

Centers for Disease Control and Prevention (CDC)
4770 Buford Hwy. NE, MS F-63, Atlanta, GA 30341-3717
(800) 232-4636 • fax: (770) 488-4760
e-mail: cdcinfo@cdc.gov
Web site: www.cdc.gov/ncipc/dvp/Suicide/

The CDC is dedicated to protecting health and promoting quality of life through the prevention and control of disease, injury, and disability. It is committed to programs that reduce the health and economic consequences of the leading causes of death and disability, including suicide. Fact sheets, reports, statistics, and podcasts are available at its Web site.

Centre for Suicide Prevention
1202 Centre St. SE, Ste. 320, Calgary, AB T2G 5A5
(403) 245-3900 • fax: (403) 245-0299
e-mail: casp@suicideinfo.ca
Web site: www.suicideinfo.ca

The Centre for Suicide Prevention comprises the Suicide Information & Education Collection (SIEC), a special library and resource center providing information on suicide and suicidal behavior; the Suicide Prevention Training Programs (SPTP), which provides caregiver training in suicide intervention, awareness, bereavement, crisis management, and related topics; and Suicide Prevention Research Projects (SPRP), which advocates for and supports research on suicide and suicidal behavior. The SIEC maintains a large library and offers document delivery services.

Indian Health Service (IHS)
The Reyes Building, 801 Thompson Ave., Ste. 400
Rockville, MD 20852-1627
Suicide Prevention Contact: (301) 443-2038
Suicide Prevention Web site: www.ihs.gov/NonMedicalPrograms/ nspn/

The purpose of the IHS Community Suicide Prevention Web site is to provide American Indian and Alaska Native communities with culturally appropriate information about best and promising practices, training opportunities, and other relevant information regarding suicide prevention and intervention. The goal of the Web site is to provide Native communities with the tools and information to create, or adapt to, their own suicide prevention programs.

International Association for Suicide Prevention (IASP)
Mrs. Vanda Scott, OBE; IASP Central Administrative Office
Le Barade F-32330 Gondrin - France
+33 562 29 19 47 • fax: +33 562 29 19 47
e-mail: iasp1960@aol.com
Web site: www.med.uio.no/iasp/

IASP is a nongovernmental organization in official relationship with the World Health Organization (WHO) concerned with suicide prevention. Founded in 1960, IASP now includes professionals and volunteers from more than fifty different countries. The organization is dedicated to preventing suicidal behavior, alleviating its effects, and providing a forum for academians, mental health professionals, crisis workers, volunteers, and suicide survivors. IASP publishes *The Journal of Crisis Intervention and Suicide Prevention*, conference papers, and resources for World Suicide Prevention Day, which it cosponsors. Online publications include titles such as *Preventing Suicide: A Resource for Media Professionals*, *How to Start a Survivors' Group*, and *Suicide and the Economic Depression: Reflections on Suicide During the Great Depression*.

The Jason Foundation Inc. (JFI)
181 E. Main St., Jefferson Bldg., Ste. 5, Hendersonville, TN 37075
e-mail: info@jasonfoundation.com
Web site: www.jasonfoundation.com

JFI programs build an awareness of the national health problem of youth suicide, educate participants in recognizing the "warning signs or signs of concern," provide information on identifying at-risk behavior and elevated risk groups, and direct participants to local resources to deal with possible suicidal ideation. It is a nationally recognized provider of educational curricula and makes available brochures and fact sheets online.

National Alliance for the Mentally Ill (NAMI)
Colonial Place Three, 2107 Wilson Blvd., Ste. 300
Arlington, VA 22201-3042
(703) 524-7600 • fax: (703) 524-9094
e-mail: www.nami.org/Template.cfm?Section=Contact_Us
Web site: www.nami.org

NAMI is a consumer advocacy and support organization composed largely of family members of people with severe mental illnesses such as schizophrenia, manic-depressive illness, and depression. The alliance adheres to the position that severe mental illnesses are biological brain diseases and that mentally ill people should not be blamed or stigmatized for their conditions. NAMI favors increased government funding for research, treatment, and community services for the mentally ill. Its publications include the bimonthly newsletter *NAMI Advocate* as well as brochures, handbooks, and policy recommendations.

National Institute of Mental Health (NIMH)
6001 Executive Blvd., Bethesda, MD 20892
(866) 615-6464 or (301) 443-4513 or (301) 443-4279
fax: 301-443-4279
e-mail: nimhinfo@nih.gov
Web site: www.nimh.nih.gov

The mission of NIMH is to transform the understanding and treatment of mental illnesses through basic and clinical research, paving the way for prevention, recovery, and cure. The NIMH publishes brochures, fact sheets, and educational curricula. Videos of selected NIMH-sponsored lectures, conferences, and presentations are available for online viewing.

National Strategy for Suicide Prevention (NSSP)
PO Box 2345, Rockville, MD 20847
toll-free: (800) 789-2647 • fax: (240) 221-4295

e-mail: http://nmhicstore.samhsa.gov/emails/
Web site: http://mentalhealth.samhsa.gov/suicideprevention/

The National Strategy for Suicide Prevention is a collaborative effort of the Substance Abuse and Mental Health Services Administration (SAMHSA), the National Institutes of Health (NIH), the Centers for Disease Control and Prevention (CDC), and the Health Resources and Services Administration (HRSA). Its Web site provides information about suicide and suicide prevention efforts.

Samaritans
Chris, PO Box 9090, Stirling, UK FK8 2SA
01753 216500 • fax: 01753 775787
e-mail: jo@samaritans.org
Web site: www.samaritans.org.uk

Samaritans is the largest suicide prevention organization in the world. Established in England in 1953, the organization now has branches in at least forty-four nations throughout the world. The group's volunteers provide counseling and other assistance to suicidal and despondent individuals. Samaritans publishes booklets such as *Youth and Self-Harm* and *Depression and Suicide,* as well as *Youth Pack*, a resource for teachers and others working with young people.

Suicide Prevention Action Network USA (SPAN USA)
1025 Vermont Ave. NW, Ste. 1066, Washington, DC 20005
(202) 449-3600 • fax: (202) 449-3601
e-mail: info@spanusa.org
Web site: www.spanusa.org

SPAN USA is a suicide-prevention organization dedicated to leveraging grassroots support among suicide survivors (those who have lost a loved one to suicide and those who have attempted suicide) and others to advance public policies that help prevent suicide. The organization was created to raise awareness, build political will, and as a call for action with regard to creating, advancing, implementing and evaluating a national strategy to address suicide. On its

Web site, SPAN USA hosts a legislative and media action center and provides brochures, newsletters, and fact sheets.

Suicide Prevention Resource Center (SPRC)
Education Development Center, Inc., 55 Chapel St.
Newton, MA 02458-1060
(877) 438-7772 • fax: (617) 969-9186
e-mail: info@sprc.org
Web site: www.sprc.org

The SPRC helps states and communities increase their capacity to develop, implement, and evaluate suicide-prevention programs. It provides technical assistance, information, resources, and training. The center is a cooperative effort between the Substance Abuse and Mental Health Services Administration and the Education Development Center. It publishes The Spark, an e-newsletter; maintains a registry of best practices; and makes freely available an extensive online library of publications.

The Trevor Project
Administrative Offices, 9056 Santa Monica Blvd., Ste. 208
West Hollywood, CA 90069
(310) 271-8845 • fax: (310) 271-8846
Help line: (866) 4-U-TREVOR or (866) 488-7386
e-mail: info@thetrevorproject.org
Web site: www.thetrevorproject.org

The Trevor Project is a nonprofit organization that operates an around-the-clock crisis and suicide-prevention help line for lesbian, gay, bisexual, transgender, and questioning (LGBTQ) youth. Each year, its help line fields more than 15,000 calls from LGBTQ youth, their families, friends, and teachers. It also educates teachers, reaches out to schools around the country, and develops relationships with organizations nationwide to better serve youth. Internet banner ads, promotional material, facts, and the *Trevor Workshop Guide* are available online at no cost. The Trevor Survival Kit and *Trevor* film are also available through the Web site.

BIBLIOGRAPHY

Books

Lisa Boesky, *When to Worry: How to Tell if Your Teen Needs Help—and What to Do About It*. New York: AMACOM, 2007.

Bev Cobain, *When Nothing Matters Anymore: A Survival Guide for Depressed Teens*. Minneapolis: Free Spirit, 2007.

Sandra Giddens, *Frequently Asked Questions About Suicide*. New York: Rosen, 2009.

Gail Griffith, *Will's Choice: A Suicidal Teen, a Desperate Mother, and a Chronicle of Recovery*. New York: HarperCollins, 2005.

Gary E. Nelson, *A Relentless Hope: Surviving the Storm of Teen Depression*. Eugene, OR: Cascade, 2007.

Richard E. Nelson, Judith C. Galas, and Pamela Espeland, *The Power to Prevent Suicide: A Guide for Teens Helping Teens*. Minneapolis: Free Spirit, 1994.

Jessica Portner, *One in Thirteen: The Silent Epidemic of Teen Suicide*. Beltsville, MD: Robin Lane's Press, 2001.

Lisa M. Schab, *Beyond the Blues: A Workbook to Help Teens Overcome Depression*. Oakland, CA: Instant Help Books, 2008.

Joyce Brennfleck Shannon, *Suicide Information for Teens: Health Tips About Suicide Causes and Prevention: Including Facts About Depression, Risk Factor, Getting Help, Survivor Support, and More*. Detroit: Omnigraphics, 2005.

Dorris S. Woods, *Breaking Point: Fighting to End America's Teenage Suicide Epidemic!* Culver City, CA: Tiger, 2006.

Periodicals

AScribe Health News Service, "Four in Ten Americans Have Been Touched by Teen Suicide; Social Stigma a Barrier to Seeking Help, New Research Shows," October 13, 2004.

———, "Teen Suicide and Antidepressants: Harvard Psychiatrists Review Black Box Warning," December 5, 2005.

Associated Press, "Guns Used More for Suicide than Murder," July 1, 2008.

Shaoni Bhattacharya, "Global Suicide Toll Exceeds War and Murder," Newscientist.com, September 8, 2004.

Donya Currie, "Teen Suicides Fall, but Rates Still High," *Nation's Health*, November 2008.

Tony Dokoupil, "Trouble in a 'Black Box'; Did an Effort to Reduce Teen Suicides Backfire?" *Newsweek*, July 16, 2007.

Mary Eberstadt, "The Family: Discovering the Obvious," *First Things*, February 2004.

Sarah Wassner Flynn, "Coming Out of the Darkness," *Girls' Life*, December 2008.

Gayle Forman, "The Tragic Mystery of Suicide," *Cosmopolitan*, May 2008.

Michelle Hainer, "The Scary Truth About Teen Suicide," *Teen People*, Sept 1, 2005.

Harvard Health Publications Group, "Program Reduces Teen Suicide Attempts," *Harvard Review of Health News*, August 21, 2006.

David Hosansky, "Youth Suicide," *CQ Researcher*, February 13, 2004.

Arlene Kaplan, "Battling a National Killer: TeenScreen Aims to Prevent Teen Suicide," *Psychiatric Times*, March 1, 2006.

Matthew Kauffman and Lisa Chedekel, "Probing the High Suicide Rate Among Soldiers in Iraq," *Nieman Reports*, Summer 2008.

Hsiang-Ching Kung, Donna L. Hoyert, Jiaquan Xu, and Sherry L. Murphy, "Deaths: Final Data for 2005," *National Vital Statistics Reports*, April 24, 2008.

Susan J. Landers, "Panel: SSRIs Don't Increase Teen Suicide Risk," *American Medical News*, February 9, 2004.

Diana Mahoney, "Teen Suicide: A Multifaceted Problem," *Clinical Psychiatry News*, December 2006.

Elizabeth Mechcatie, "FDA Panels Back Black Box for Antidepressants: Support for Strongest Warning Is Based on a 'Reasonably Consistent Signal for Risk,'" *Pediatric News*, October 2004.

Medical Letters on the CDC & FDA, "Research Reveals Social Isolation Boosts Teen Girls' Suicide Thoughts," January 25, 2004.

Lisa Neef, "A Portrait of Pain," *The Advocate*, March 2, 2004.

Patrice G.W. Norton, "Prevention Plan Reduces Teen Suicide Attempts," *Clinical Psychiatry News*, May 2004.

Robert M. O'Neil, "It's Not Easy to Stand Up to Cyberbullies, but We Must," *Chronicle of Higher Education*, July 11, 2008.

Benjamin Radford, "Suicide More Common than Homicide," *LiveScience.com*, August 29, 2007.

Julie Rawe and Kathleen Kingsbury, "When Colleges Go on Suicide Watch," *Time*, May 22, 2006.

Michele G. Sullivan, "Recognize Risk Factors in Teen Suicide Attempters: Presence of Psychiatric Illness, Preparedness for the Suicidal Act Increase Patient's Likelihood of Repeat," *Clinical Psychiatry News*, January 2004.

E.M. Swift, "What Went Wrong in Winthrop?" *Sports Illustrated*, January 9, 2006.

Marianne Szgedy-Maszak, "Medication & Melancholy," *U.S. News & World Report*, May 16, 2005.

Violence Policy Center, "American Roulette: Murder-Suicide in the United States, Third Edition," Washington, DC: Violence Policy Center, April 2008.

W. Bradford Wilcox, "Children at Risk," *First Things*, February 2004.

Duff Wilson, "Steroids: One Teen's Tale: Efrain Marrero Wanted to Bulk Up for Football. After His Death, at 19, Steroids Are Called the Culprit," *New York Times Upfront*, September 19, 2005.

Eilene Zimmerman, "Teen Angst Turns Deadly: Why Girls Are Killing Themselves," *Psychology Today*, January 2009.

INDEX

Meier, Ron, 63, 66
Meier, Tina, 66
Mood disorders, 27, 31
Morris, Laura, 85

N
National Center for Injury Prevention and Control, 81
National Institutes of Mental Health (NIMH), 39
National Suicide Prevention Lifeline, 77, 78–79
Native American teens, 18–23, *22*
The New Gay Teenager (Savin-Williams), 15–16

O
O'Brien, Thomas, 61, 62, 63–64, 65
Office of Indian Education Programs (OIEP), 21, 22–23

P
Parry, Anne, 33
Patrick, Robert, 61
The Pawnbroker (film), 25
Post-traumatic stress disorder (PTSD), 27–28
Poulten, Meredith, 83
Prevention/prevention programs, 72
  aimed at Native American youth, 21–23
  crisis hotlines, 74–79
  in high schools, 80–85
Project Cornerstone, 52

R
Randall, Natasha, 32, 34
Robbins, Charles, 14–15
Roberts, Selena, 50
Rummel, Heidi, 66
Ryan, Caitlin, 17

S
Salavar, Jesus, 50, 51–52, 52–53
Savin-Williams, Ritch, 15–16
Selective serotonin reuptake inhibitors (SSRIs), 39
  have done more good than harm, 43
  side effects of, 41–42
Signs of Suicide (SOS) prevention program, 80–81, 83–84
  outcomes of, *82*
Singer, Marti, 71
Smith, Cathy, 57, 59, 60
Stewart, Dean, 63, 66
Substance abuse, 26, 27
Substance Abuse and Mental Health Services Administration, 81
Suicide Clusters (Coleman), 35
Suicide/suicide rates
  adolescent literature addressing, *70*
  among adolescents, 48
  by age group and ethnicity, *22*
  attempted/considered, 9
  clusters, 32–36
  influence of media on, *37*
  for LGBT adolescents, 9

in Native American youth, *22*

numbers among soldiers on active duty, *26*

prevalence of, *74, 79*

by state, *76*

warning signs of, *68*

young unmarried soldiers are at greater risk for, *24–31*

Surveys, *14, 19, 51*

Survivor guilt, *25*

T

Taylor, Mark, *38, 39*

Teachers, *58–60, 68–73*

Teen suicide

antidepressants contribute to increase in, *38–43*

clusters of, *35–36*

cyberbullies and, *55–60, 61–66*

cyberbullying can lead to, *50–54*

desire for attention as motivate for, *32–37*

factors contributing to increase in, *12, 18*

high school programs can help prevent, *80–85*

is a significant problem, *8–12*

open communication and, *67–73*

Tracy, Ann Blake, *39*

Trevor Project, *14*

V

Valentino, Marilyn, *71*

W

Washington Post (newspaper), *45, 49*

Weir, Kirsten, *38*

When Not to Keep a Secret (American Psychiatric Association Alliance), *72*

Whirligig (Fleischman), *70–71*

Willard, Nancy, *58, 60*

Y

Yellow Ribbon Campaign, *72*

Youth Risk Behavior Surveys (YRBS), *14, 19*

PICTURE CREDITS